Playing Tennis

24008

PLAYING TENNIS

Sue
Barker

TAPLINGER PUBLISHING COMPANY
NEW YORK

First published in the United States in 1980 by
TAPLINGER PUBLISHING CO., INC.
New York, New York

Library of Congress Catalog Card Number: 79–66012
ISBN 0–8008–6323–2

Contents

Introduction

For just about as long as I can remember tennis has been my life, and it continues to be not only my method of earning a living but a game which I continue to enjoy, despite the tremendous amount of travelling and living out of a suitcase, and the fact that I have to spend too much time away from England these days.

Through this book I would like to invite you to share with me my enjoyment of what I consider the world's finest sport. I must assume that you are interested in tennis, otherwise this book wouldn't be in your hands right now! My intention is to stimulate that interest and attempt to ensure that you *stay* interested in the game by helping you to improve your tennis or, if you are a beginner, to assist you along the right path towards a sound technique.

My next assumption is that you are fairly familiar with the rules of tennis, and how it is played. In other words, that you know the difference between a ground stroke and a volley, the difference between 'love' and 'deuce'.

In order to play tennis well it is important, rather like a house, to have good foundations. Learn to walk before you run, and learn to run before you swing the racket. To put it another way, advance with small steps and avoid the easy pitfall of over-ambition as you attempt to master the strokes and techniques.

If you are a complete beginner you will quickly join millions of other fanatics in learning that tennis not an easy game to play. It demands a good sense of co-ordination — and it is surprising how many people lack this valuable asset. Natural athletes, or people already skilled at other ball games, may find it difficult to understand that some folk have problems hitting a moving object while they themselves are on the move.

Such people will take comfort from the old saying that success at tennis is 90 per cent perspiration and 10 per cent inspiration. There is no doubt that you can overcome — with enough determination, practice and will to win — the obvious early hurdles in your path. Your attitude towards physical fitness is an example. Most young people ought to be in good shape, although a couple of hours spent charging around a tennis court on a hot day will quickly show just *how* good a shape you are in.

Fitness is a target which can be achieved, and maintained of course, with nothing more than the correct attitude and the right amount of determination — the knowledge, for instance, that you really should go out for a jog in the cold weather or do some skipping exercises in the back yard rather than relax in front of a TV set or stereo deck.

This is all part of what I would term the proper mental approach to your game, the vital attitude that you want to be better at tennis. It's an outlook which I still have; I still want to improve my game, to work on it, to enjoy it. If you don't enjoy it, pack up and try another sport, but I defy most people *not* to enjoy tennis and the social life that surrounds it.

Although facilities in Britain are nowhere near as extensive and sophisticated as the United States — where it is estimated that the number of people who play tennis is not far short of the whole population of this country — there are plenty of good clubs able to take on keen and willing new members. There are also outdoor public courts which are relatively inexpensive and, most important, there is nowadays an increasing tendency to teach tennis as part of the sports curriculum in some schools.

There is nothing better than taking part in the weekend activities at a tennis club, and though the ability to mix well on these occasions is important (by which I mean not being afraid to play against someone who is better than you, or refusing to partner someone weaker than yourself) tennis also offers plenty of opportunities for the loner to get on with his or her climb up the ladder. If you want to practise at all hours, do so. If you can't get onto a court, or find someone willing to hit the ball back to you, there is always a convenient wall off which you can bounce your shots as you relieve the loneliness by imagining that you have just struck a devastating ground stroke past Bjorn Borg or Martina Navratilova!

In these pages I have attempted to explain, in as simple and straightforward a manner as possible, how to execute the basic strokes of the game. In other words, how the shots *ought* to be played. But it is a great truism to say that there is no *one* way to play tennis. Individual quirks, preferences and strengths (and weaknesses!) vitally affect every single person who wields a racket. For instance, it may not have escaped your attention if you have watched me in action that I have a strong liking for my forehand, for the simple reason that it earns me a lot of points. In order to hit winners I sometimes resort to the unorthodox, such as running round the ball to get it onto my forehand, and as far as I'm concerned this is perfectly acceptable as long as it wins points.

The dangers of this sort of thing are explained in the chapters on technique, strategy and attitudes towards the game. All these are just as important as the art of stroke making if you want to make a success of your tennis.

Finally, I must apologise to the 10 per cent or so of tennis players who are left-handed. It would be too complicated and lengthy to explain every single piece of advice in this book twice over. But don't regard yourselves as a suffering minority; little more is usually needed than a simple transposition — left to right or vice versa — to make the transition workable. Or, if that is complicated, stand in front of a full-length mirror to practise your swing and strokes and you'll see what I mean.

So, as you prepare to tackle tennis the Sue Barker way, keep in mind these basic suggestions. Always try to be bold and positive in your play, but not at the expense of your accuracy. Be patient when you need to be. Never be tentative, and never, *never* argue or lose your temper on court. Tennis is a marvellous game. Enjoy it.

1. Fitness and Training

Fitness is the first, vital key to playing better tennis and for beginners it is equally important to be in good condition when you take up the game. Your goal can be summed up in five words — get fit and stay fit — because poor conditioning will be costly in a long, gruelling match.

Jogging has become an extremely popular pastime and it is an excellent way of getting yourself in shape because it develops stamina and strengthens the legs. To get fitter you have to get the heart rate up, you have to push yourself, and jogging is ideal for this. You have to learn to push yourself a little more every time you go out for a run. The responsibility is on you, *and nobody else*, to shave a few more seconds off your time round the local park or even round your housing estate or city block.

I jogged for years when I was starting out and I still go for a run sometimes, though nowadays I have other ways of keeping in shape which I prefer. I quite like to jog, especially if I have someone to join me on the run, but I have never enjoyed jogging on my own. If I've got someone to run with me, that's fine. Otherwise, I'm afraid I get bored. But that's not the way a lot of people look at it, thank goodness!

When I'm travelling, which is most of the time these days, I do daily exercises in my hotel room, or wherever I am staying, stretching and warming up to the 'popmobility' records devised by Ken Woolcott. These records are available at many record shops, and if you don't happen to have access to a record player you can always tape them and play them on a portable tape recorder wherever you happen to be when you want to spend a few minutes exercising and getting into shape.

But there are a number of good, simple conditioning exercises you can perform which, if done for a few minutes every morning when you get up and, if possible, for another short spell in the evening, will work wonders in toning up the muscles and building stamina.

Simple sit-ups, a few press-ups, toe touching from a seated position and trunk pivotal exercises are excellent, and if the weather outside is too miserable to consider jogging, then try a little running on the spot.

A set of chest expanders, easily and inexpensively purchased from a sports shop, are also recommended for youths and men, since they develop the chest, encourage deep breathing and also pull in the stomach. For girls and women who have slighter bodies and smaller shoulders and are therefore generally more limited in their overhead game, there are com-

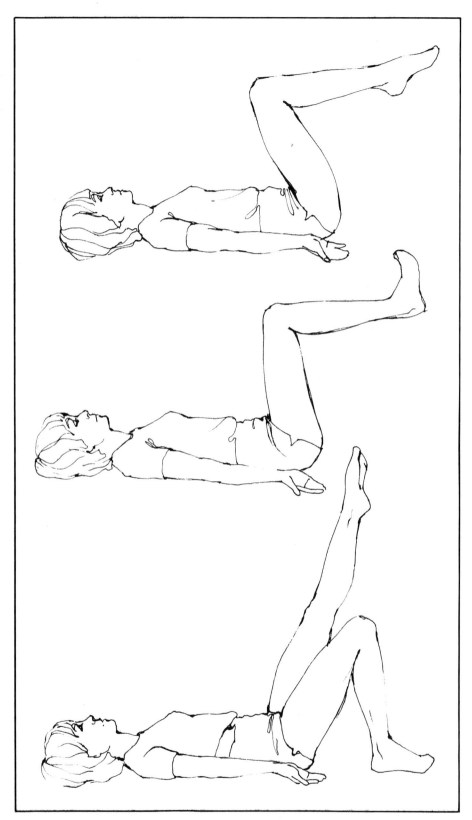

Figure 1 A good conditioning exercise. Lie flat with knees flexed, shins parallel to the floor and backs of hands on ground. Lower right leg to floor and extend left leg upwards. Slowly raise right leg and lower the left. Repeat about ten times. Stretch both legs together towards the ceiling then bring legs back to starting position. Raise left leg, right foot on floor, rotate left ankle completing five full circles, then rotate complete leg five times. Repeat exercise with the other leg.

12

pensating conditioning exercises which develop the ability to move more easily from side to side, an essential factor in playing the baseline game.

Lie flat on the floor on your back with your knees flexed above the hips and lower legs also parallel to the floor (as in fig. 1). Then pull first your right knee, then the left, towards your shoulders. It's excellent for tightening the abdominal muscles. Try it a dozen times, and gradually try to build up the number. At all times keep the back and shoulders firmly pressed against the floor, with the arms parallel to the body, fully extended and with the palms of the hands uppermost.

There are other variations of this abdominal exercise, such as extending your left and right legs alternately towards the ceiling, and then pushing out both legs together up into the air.

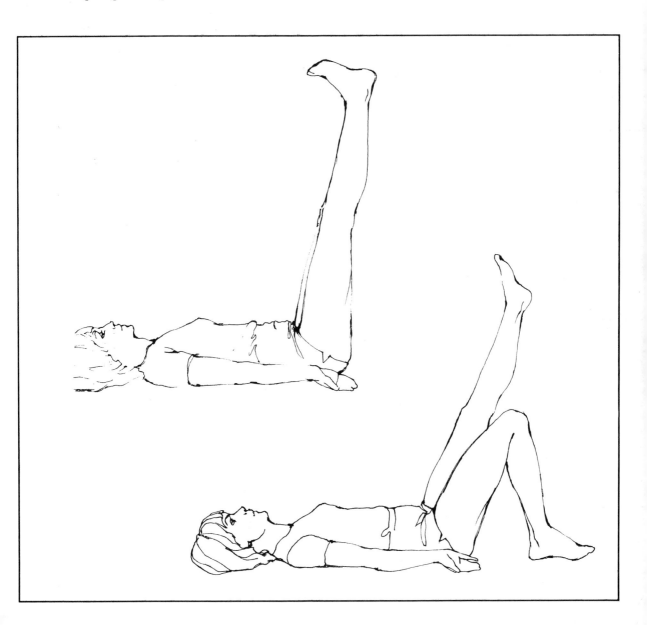

My favourite exercise is skipping, and I carry a skipping rope with me everywhere I travel. Skipping is better than anything else I know for keeping you on your toes, and it can be fun reviving the rhymes and rhythms of childhood days.

Skipping and short sprints are what I concentrate on mainly, because I am basically a baseline player which means I have to scamper a lot more than someone who plays the serve and volley type of tennis. So fitness is very important to me, since I don't possess a big serve and I'm not going to win a lot of points merely by being powerful. I need to run a lot of balls down and fitness is vital, so that's why I prefer skipping and short sprints.

Other racket games, such as squash and badminton are very good for building up stamina and sharpening the reflexes, and preferable to things like weight training. They are also good for eye/ball co-ordination.

A lot of people go too far the other way in chasing fitness and spend more time doing exercises at the expense of time spent on court. This was a mistake I made when I was about 14 years old. I did a lot of training and only played about two hours a day — although I realise that this is more than most people are able to devote to tennis when it is only a pastime. But it's important not to let training interfere with your on-court activities, because that's where the best fitness of all is achieved. A sensible programme of stamina building is obviously excellent, but *not* as a replacement for actually playing the game.

Another important thing to remember is always to practise stretching the body muscles before practice or before a game to warm yourself up and prevent injury and strains.

It's a very good idea before you play to run around the court ten times to boost your fitness rate and get the body working. The worst thing you can do is start a match from 'cold'. Yet I see so many people doing this. They would get so much more out of the game if they warmed up before they started their match. It costs nothing, it's easy to do and it is so beneficial. Any exercise is good, as long as it makes you feel warm.

One very good exercise which you can actually do on court with the assistance of a friend is to place six balls on one side of the service line, another six on the other side of the service line some distance away and six more in a group at the net.

You designate each bunch of balls 'one', 'two' and 'three', and then go and stand at the centre of the baseline, with your friend standing behind you. He or she will then shout out a number — for instance 'one', and you have to dash forward, pick up a ball from that group, then run backwards and place it on the baseline. It is just like running forward to reach a short ball returned by your opponent. Then they shout 'three' and you immediately sprint to the net, pick up a ball and once again run backwards to the baseline. And so on, until all eighteen balls have been collected.

The important thing is that you don't know where you are going to have to run until you get the call. Anything such as that which involves quick movement is very good, and the best place to do it is on court because it gets you accustomed to the size and area of a tennis court.

It is also essential to strengthen the wrists, and these exercises can be done at quiet moments during the day at school or at work simply by repeatedly squeezing a small rubber ball like a squash ball or using a wrist-

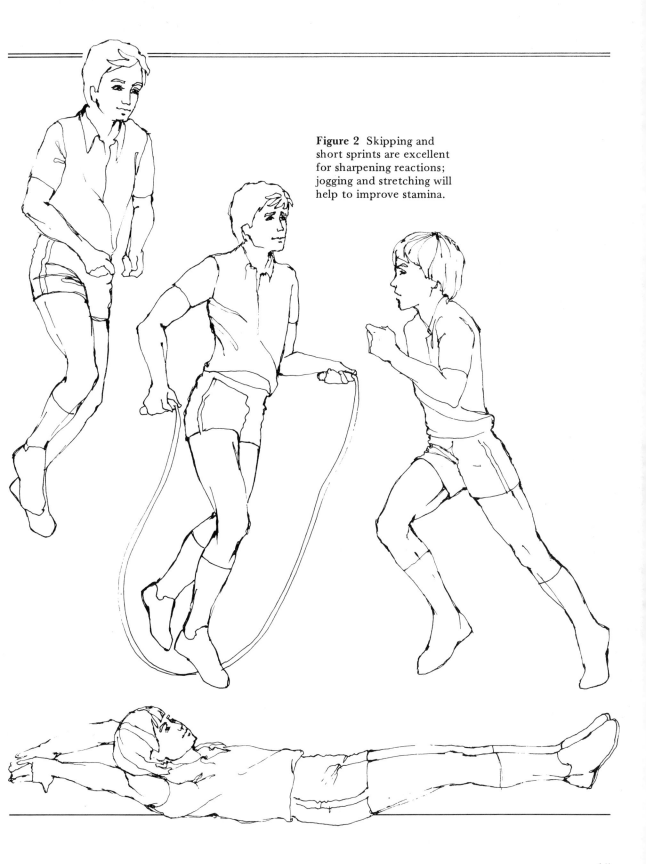

Figure 2 Skipping and short sprints are excellent for sharpening reactions; jogging and stretching will help to improve stamina.

building aid, such as the ones marketed to help golfers.

But perhaps the best exercise for this is just to bounce a ball on a racket, switching alternately from one side of the racket to the other. Not only does this strengthen the wrist but it ensures that you watch the ball onto your racket, and is excellent for co-ordination. When you have a racket and a ball in your hands you somehow feel that you're doing it all for tennis, not just for the sake of your wrist! It's important to *enjoy* whatever you are doing, whether it be exercises, practice or playing. Then you will improve.

Meal planning is also an important part of your exercise preparation. There is a saying 'you are what you eat' and in tennis this could be extended: also 'you are what you drink'.

I realise that this cannot apply to every club player, of course, but I cannot eat less than four hours before I am due to play because for one thing I get nervous and I'm not hungry, and for another I can't run on a full stomach. My coach at Torquay, Arthur Roberts, always told me it is better just to feel a little hungry when you walk on court. It makes your mind sharper and more active. It also makes you hungrier for the match, too.

Juniors eat so many chocolate bars and things before they go on court and although chocolate is very nutritious it sits in the bottom of your stomach and doesn't really make you feel good. If you are hungry before going out to play it is best just to have a couple of biscuits, or something like that. If you have to wait an unexpected extra half-hour before playing and you become really hungry a biscuit will take away the edge of hunger. Fruit isn't very good for this sort of occasion.

As far as liquid is concerned, sugar-content drinks are good to take before playing. I just drink regular orange squash. It is important to drink a lot because it is surprising just how much liquid you lose from your body when you're practising and playing. I have been caught three or four times a little dehydrated, and it brings on headaches and breaks your concentration. So, even if you don't really feel like it before a match, you should always try to drink a little something — not alcohol, of course, and even if you are very hot it is not advisable to drink iced water because that can give you stomach cramps. I've had it and I warn you, it's terrible. It really is!

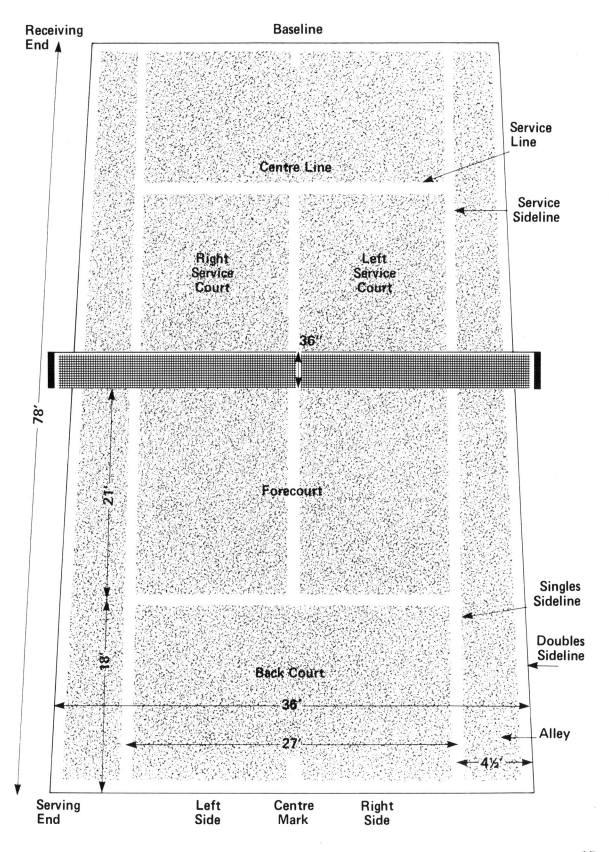

Receiving End

Baseline

Service Line

Service Sideline

Centre Line

Right Service Court

Left Service Court

36"

21'

Forecourt

18'

Singles Sideline

Doubles Sideline

Back Court

36'

27'

4½'

Alley

78'

Serving End

Left Side

Centre Mark

Right Side

17

2. Equipment

There are two really important items of equipment over which you need to expend time, care and money when you take up tennis: a racket and a pair of shoes. Other items of clothing and equipment are not so important but, like the racket and the shoes, they will also need to feel comfortable and easy to play in.

Comfort is the first thing you should look for when you pick up a racket. Does it *feel* comfortable in your hand? Is the grip comfortable? People can advise you for ever about what sort of grip and handle width you need, but only you will know if it feels right. Here's one basic piece of advice to help in your choice: when you pick up the racket, the fingers should almost touch the fleshy part of the palm beneath the thumb. If your fingers and your palm are touching, the handle is too narrow for you. If the two parts of your hand are a long way apart and the racket feels unwieldy when you try to swing it, then the handle is too thick for your purposes.

In choosing your racket, select a reputable manufacturer. I use a Slazenger Challenge Number One. Its dependability has been proven over the years and, most important, it is available in a wide range of sizes, weights and balances. There is a junior version of the Challenge Number One for the young beginners, which ensures that you can retain the same type of racket, and the familiarity with it, as your game develops and you get a little older and bigger. It is important that children should be able to play with the proper weight racket. That way they will enjoy their first experience of tennis.

When I started to play I had to use a full size racket and for about two years I was really struggling. You don't enjoy your tennis when you are struggling. If the racket is too heavy for you, the head will drop — and this is one of the most serious flaws in stroke making. In other words, too heavy a racket is a serious handicap from the start and could lead you into bad habits.

Having said that, I should also point out that the racket should be as heavy as feels comfortable to swing. When learning the game your ground strokes need to be flat and conventional and in order to achieve this your racket should be heavy enough to do the work for you when you swing at the ball. If the racket is too light you could develop the equally bad habit of flicking at the ball.

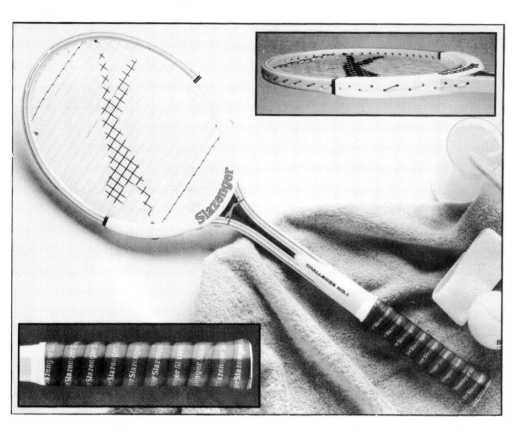

The increasing use of synthetic materials, such as aluminium, steel, fibreglass and graphite which are less dense than wood is leading to lighter rackets. In addition, this type of synthetic racket is stronger than wood, so it usually has a smaller cross section and gives less resistance when it is being swung.

It is useful not to have too much weight in the head, for instance, if you suddenly have to move your racket, for example from the backhand position to the forehand volley while moving in to the net. The average racket weight used to be about 13¾ oz, but this has now come down to under 13¼ oz, which is the average weight. They are even made under 13 oz nowadays.

If you are learning the basics of tennis, however, make certain that your racket head is neither too light nor too heavy. While it is true that rackets made of steel, aluminium etc. enable you to generate more power and whip on the ball, these rackets tend to be very expensive. And, as I have pointed out, wood is excellent and dependable. I use one myself.

A lot of professionals who switched to the new materials when they first came in have now gone back to wooden rackets. A point you might bear in mind if some of the weird and wonderful looking rackets used by pros tend to impress you, is that they are being paid to use them and they may not be what they would use as their first preference. I know that I tried a fibreglass racket at one stage but soon reverted to wood.

The other great advantage of a wooden racket is that you can adjust the shape and size of the handle by having a bit shaved off if necessary or building it up.

The handle, the point of contact with the racket, is where the player makes — or attempts to make — it all happen. This is why it is imperative that the grip should be comfortable. Get a racket with a soft calf leather handle if possible. There are various methods of ensuring that your grip on that handle is firm and not slippery. You can carry a small amount of sawdust in your pocket and rub it on the handle between points to absorb moisture. A small towel tucked into the waistband will achieve the same effect. There is also a resin bag on the market now which helps to obtain a firmer grip. And if you run into trouble during a match, there is a self-adhesive tape which can be rapidly and easily wrapped around the handle if you are having problems with your grip.

While on the subject of handle grip, it is important to remind you to take good care of both your hands and feet. If they aren't looked after properly you could pay the penalty of having to default a match or not being able to play tennis because of blisters or split fingers. If you develop hard pads on hands or feet, pare them down with the sort of instrument you can buy from foot care shops. If you let the hard pad build up too much there is a risk that you may find a blister forming beneath the callous. People build up hard skin at different rates, according to their metabolism and skin type. If you tend to suffer from split fingers wrap adhesive tape around the most exposed fingers, either to stop this happening or as a precaution against it happening.

Another way of keeping the skin soft is by using Melrose. This comes in tablet-shape and is rubbed into the skin to prevent it from cracking. In cold weather cracked skin can be a constant source of irritation.

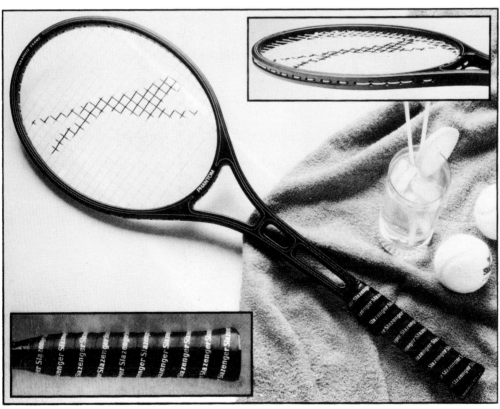

A selection of senior, junior and specialised matchplay rackets.

Now to the question of what type of stringing you should have in your racket. In my opinion beginners certainly don't need anything more than a good quality synthetic string. It is appreciably cheaper than gut and lasts twice as long. It's a paradox about tennis strings that the more you pay for them the shorter time they will last. The advantage that gut has over synthetic materials is that you obtain greater 'feel' and resilience in your stroke making. So the time to move on to gut is when you have mastered the basics of the technique and when you feel that fineness of touch matters enough to pay extra for it. In the meantime, save money and use synthetic strings. There is the added factor that they are not affected by moisture, as gut undoubtedly is.

A lot of people believe, quite wrongly, that your racket needs to be strung terribly tight in order to make you play better. Not so. Tight strings give you less control, and less control means more errors. The normal racket tension is around 56 lb. There are some professionals who prefer their rackets more tightly strung. Bjorn Borg is the best example. His are board hard, about 70 lbs, which means that his timing has to be razor sharp.

Normal, or even slightly slack, stringing, allows the ball to sink into the strings on contact, and to stay on the strings just that fraction of a second longer, giving very good control.

With shoes, like rackets, comfort is the primary question. The shoe must fit snugly, preferably over one pair of woolen socks. If your foot can move around inside the shoe you will suffer, because blisters are formed by the rubbing action of foot moving on sock, and sock moving around inside shoe. You should not need to wear a second pair of socks if the shoe is the correct fitting, but I know a lot of players who are happier wearing two pairs. In fact Kerry Reid wears four pairs!

I prefer a canvas tennis shoe to a leather one. In leather I tend to get more blisters, and I find a canvas shoe 'breathes' more readily. On the other hand a leather shoe lasts a lot longer for the extra money. Comfort and personal preference is the decider here, really. I know of people who prefer leather because it gives them better ankle support. So pay your money, take your choice. But remember, wear a new pair of tennis shoes around the house and outside as a means of breaking them in slightly before you play in them.

As with rackets, don't stint on quality in your choice of shoes. There is a wide variety of makes available from reputable manufacturers. Don't be tempted to get such-and-such a make because so-and-so wears them. It makes much more sense to find a shoe which fits the size and *shape* of your feet.

Before playing, always lace up your shoes tightly to prevent that foot movement which can lead to blisters, and always make sure your laces are in good repair. Never go out on court with a suspect lace. If it breaks in the middle of a match it could cause you to lose your concentration — and possibly your temper.

With the rest of your clothing — dresses, shirts, shorts and under-clothing, make sure that what you are wearing was designed for tennis and that you can stretch inside it. Here again, comfort is essential and it is important that any foot or leg movement should not be impeded by ill-fitting gear. Also, buy the sort of material which washes easily and is drip dry. Then you can wash your clothes through, hang them up over-night and have them ready for use again the next day.

A slipover, or sleeveless sweater, is a useful item in uncertain climates. It keeps the back protected, and you can play in it quite comfortably if the weather is chilly. You could also play in your track suit if the weather is decidedly unfriendly. Here again, try to ensure that the quality is good, that it keeps you warm and does not restrict arm or leg movement.

Finally, a word about racket care. These days a well-made racket, provided it is not stored near a radiator or exposed to excessive changes of temperature or humidity, does not need to be kept in a press. When you break a string, however, you should have it repaired immediately or cut the other strings to relieve the uneven pressure on the racket frame.

Many people fail to realise that severe damage can be done to a racket in a very few days if a broken string is left unrepaired. Cutting the other strings might seem a severe way of dealing with the problem but it is better than trying to play with a cracked or deformed racket.

Head covers are a useful item in the maintenance of your racket. They help to keep rain and other moisture away from the strings, but be careful to dry off any moisture which may have accumulated on the strings before you put the racket inside the cover, or it will sweat inside its cover and if the strings happen to be gut they will break.

Head covers, made in an attractive variety of colours and designs, are also useful when you are not keeping your racket dry. They can be pressed into service as a pouch for your valuables when you go on court, removing the need for you to leave purses and wallets in a dressing room where they might be at risk.

3. The Grip

Once you have obtained a racket that provides you with a comfortable grip, the next thing to sort out is how to hold the racket in order best to strike the ball. There are three basic styles of grip — the eastern, continental, and western. To understand how the grips differ you should study the accompanying illustrations and the diagram of the various angles of the racket.

Beginners, particularly youngsters who aren't very strong, should start with the eastern forehand and backhand grips. The eastern grip is so called because it came into popular use on the clay courts in the eastern part of the United States, which provide a comfortable bounce. The forehand grip is achieved by grasping the handle of the racket as if you were shaking hands with someone. In more technical terms, the heel of the right hand should rest on the right bevel of the handle and the thumb pad on the front panel. Then simply close the fingers round the racket.

The eastern backhand grip is obtained by rotating the hand a quarter of a turn to the left, or anti-clockwise, so that the thumb can give a little support to the backhand stroke. The heel of the hand should have moved over to the left bevel and the thumb should be lying diagonally across the front panel.

Although the grip shift is not a big one when you are changing from a forehand stroke to a backhand, you should practise the change until it becomes a natural part of your preparation to play the stroke. In other words, you shouldn't need to look at your hand to see if it is in the correct position. The feel alone should tell you, leaving your eyes to concentrate, as they should be doing, on the ball.

Most people learn to play using the eastern grip but as they make progress and become stronger, they find the need for an all-purpose grip. And since there isn't time to indulge in a grip change, such as the eastern requires, they develop the one-grip concept. In other words, the continental grip. So called because it originated on the low-bouncing clay courts of Europe, the continental grip is used by about 90 per cent of the men professionals since only the slightest adjustments is needed to play either a forehand or backhand stroke, though fewer women use it because their game is a little slower, giving time to change grips.

You achieve the continental grip by grasping the racket from above, with the heel of the hand on the top panel, the thumb extended under-

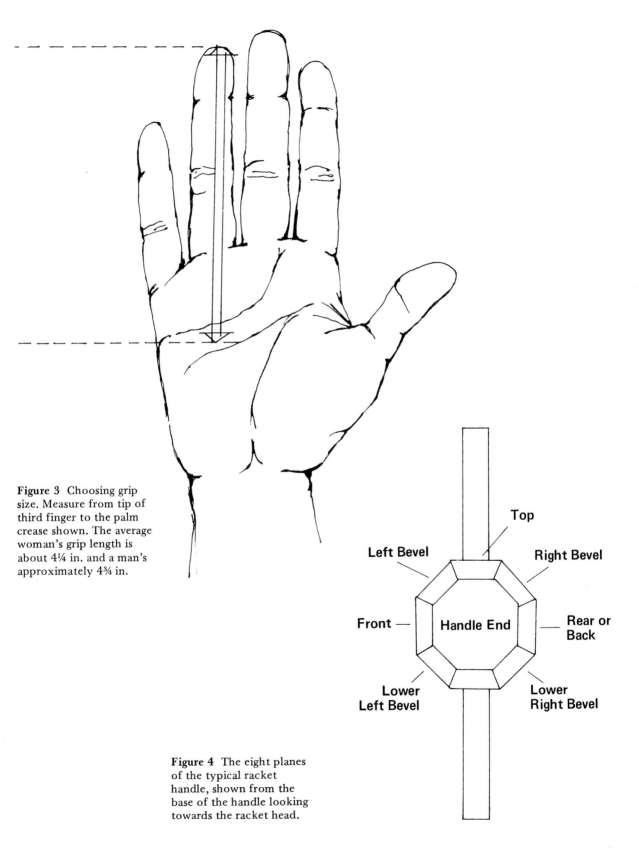

Figure 3 Choosing grip size. Measure from tip of third finger to the palm crease shown. The average woman's grip length is about 4¼ in. and a man's approximately 4¾ in.

Figure 4 The eight planes of the typical racket handle, shown from the base of the handle looking towards the racket head.

Left Bevel

Top

Right Bevel

Front —

Handle End

Rear or Back

Lower Left Bevel

Lower Right Bevel

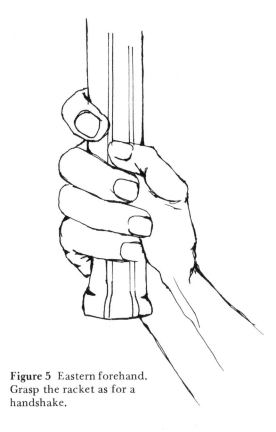

Figure 5 Eastern forehand.
Grasp the racket as for a
handshake.

neath the handle and the base knuckle of the forefinger on the right
bevel. The continental is also the standard service grip, so the grip becomes a simpler matter as your tennis improves and you become strong
enough to use only the one grip. But beginners must face up to the fact
that they must serve with the continental grip, then quickly adjust to
either an eastern forehand or backhand, until they get stronger in the
wrist. The strength of wrist required, and the more precise timing needed
in the continental grip, mean that the eastern grip is the favourite for the
ordinary or average player.

The western grip was developed in California, where the cement courts
give a high bounce, and as such is rarely used in this country, except
possibly by those who possess a double-handed backhand. By placing
the free hand on the racket for the backstroke, they don't need to change
their grip from the forehand position. The western grip is not really
suited for low bounces, as the hand is holding the racket underneath.
The heel of the hand and the base knuckle should be on the lower right
bevel, and the thumb pad on the top panel.

A slight variation of this grip, in which the heel of the hand and the
forefinger's base knuckle are on the back panel and the thumb on the
left bevel, is the grip most favoured by self-taught or unskilled players.
For the backhand western grip, the thumb is extended straight along the
front panel, the base knuckle rests on the top panel and the heel of the
hand fits along the left bevel.

26

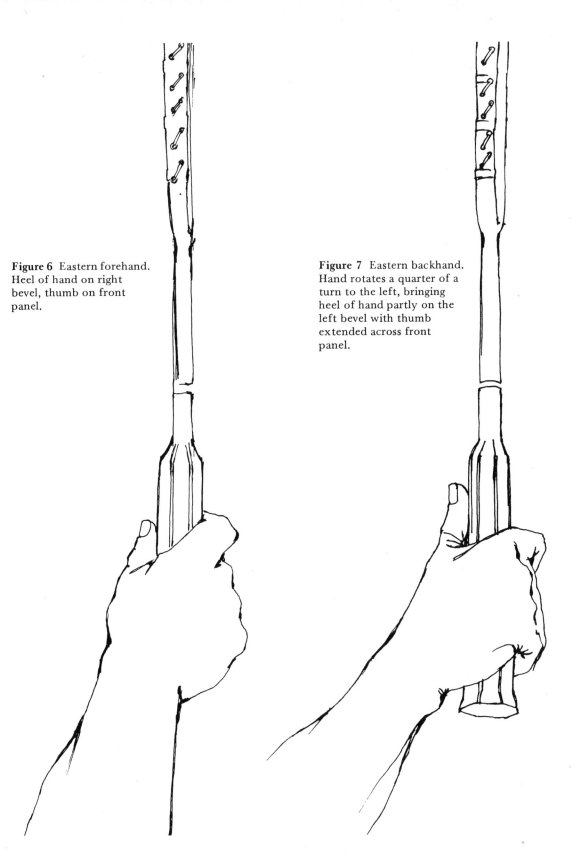

Figure 6 Eastern forehand. Heel of hand on right bevel, thumb on front panel.

Figure 7 Eastern backhand. Hand rotates a quarter of a turn to the left, bringing heel of hand partly on the left bevel with thumb extended across front panel.

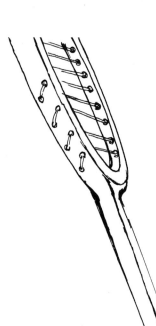

My basic advice is to stick with the eastern grips but no matter which grip you favour, remember that none of them will be the slightest use unless you grip the racket firmly enough to feel the pressure of your fingers around the handle.

Figure 8 Continental grip. Heel of hand on top panel, thumb extended underneath hand.

4. Service

When you are serving you are given a unique opportunity to dominate that particular rally from the first ball. Nothing your opponent can do can affect your ability to deliver the shot, but it is the most complex stroke in the game and the one that allows the greatest range of personal quirks and preferences, being tailored to a person's height, strength and build. For instance, tall people usually have better serves because when they throw the ball up they can obtain a steeper trajectory on the stroke.

It is vital to keep a consistently good length into the service box. To me, placement is much more important than power. Attempting to serve too hard is a common error. The first serve is so important, yet far too many people waste it by trying to hit an ace.

Even people like Bjorn Borg will serve only about four aces in a match. OK, that's four points, but would-be imitators could end up losing about 20 points by lobbing up a pathetic second serve.

It is vitally important to get your first service into court. It doesn't *have* to be a great one. The more you study the game the more you realise this. As an example, in all the big matches I have won I have had 70 per cent or more of my first serves in.

Like me, a lot of the leading women players have good serves, but by no means the best in the game. Virginia Wade has a terrific serve, of course, it wins her a lot of points and sets her up with a lot of easy second shots. In that respect it is obviously very important to her. But for someone like me, who does not normally come in to volley behind my serve, it is not such a big deal to get a *big* first serve in, but rather to ensure that the serve is good and deep. It must always be a positive shot, however. You have got to know where you intend to hit the serve before you step up to take your position on the baseline.

The first important thing to organise on your service game is what we call a 'grooved' swing, which means getting into a set pattern for serving which you repeat time after time until it becomes automatic, like many other day-to-day actions.

If beginners don't possess good timing on their serve they might try what I did when I started to play. I spent a whole year serving from a set position with the racket already poised behind my head. In other words I didn't even bother with the swing but just concentrated on getting used to hitting the ball with the correct timing.

When that timing is perfected you can then start to develop your swing. As I have already said, the serve is an extremely individualistic stroke; some people like short swings, others prefer long, loopy ones. It is purely a case of experimenting until you settle on the one that suits you best.

Now let's deal with the various elements of the serve. First, and most important, the stance. In singles play, you can choose to stand as close as possible to the centre mark on the baseline since this represents the shortest distance between your serve and the opposing service court, or

Serving: The complete service action from the start position with weight forward, into the high toss, meeting the ball cleanly at the top of the racket arc and the full and forcing follow through.

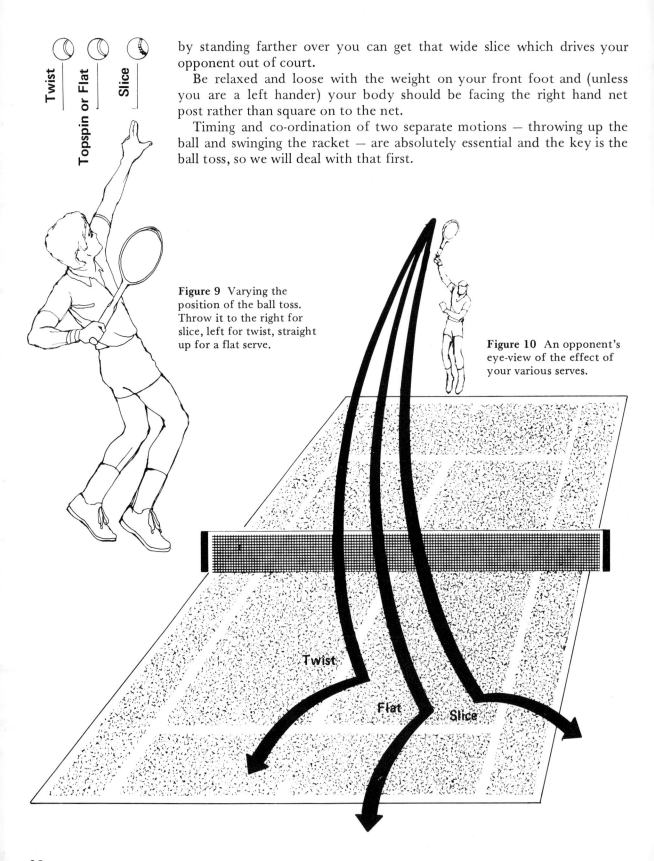

Twist | Topspin or Flat | Slice

by standing farther over you can get that wide slice which drives your opponent out of court.

Be relaxed and loose with the weight on your front foot and (unless you are a left hander) your body should be facing the right hand net post rather than square on to the net.

Timing and co-ordination of two separate motions — throwing up the ball and swinging the racket — are absolutely essential and the key is the ball toss, so we will deal with that first.

Figure 9 Varying the position of the ball toss. Throw it to the right for slice, left for twist, straight up for a flat serve.

Figure 10 An opponent's eye-view of the effect of your various serves.

Twist

Flat

Slice

Like the other parts of the service action, the toss must become automatic. How you throw the ball into the air determines to a great extent how hard and how accurately you hit it, and how well you serve.

The ball should be released when your arm is fully extended, not thrown from in front of your face, as you need to obtain the maximum height available.

To obtain a uniform toss a good exercise is to stand on the baseline without your racket, and simply throw up a ball and see where it bounces. It should bounce two feet in front of and a little to the right hand side of a right hander. If it's bouncing on top of your head then you are doing it wrong! Keep repeating the exercise until you can ensure that the ball falls on the same spot 20 successive times. Then you will know you have got the direction of the throw-up right.

Some players and coaches advise that you should only be holding one ball, rather than two, when you serve, on the grounds that if your first serve goes in you must either discard the second ball or play the point carrying it in your hand. I always serve with two balls in my left hand, it doesn't bother me at all, but obviously players who employ the two-handed backhand would be in trouble since they need both hands for their stroke.

The alternative is to put the second ball in your trouser pocket, tuck it up your skirt, or, like Tracy Austin, sew a pocket onto your dress. If holding onto the second ball interferes with your concentration or comfort, then find other ways of accommodating the ball or just pick up one at a time. It is essential for your play to feel comfortable.

As you begin the ball toss, move your weight onto the back foot, co-ordinating the movement of the right-arm racket swing and the left-arm toss. As your left arm is thrust upwards your right arm should be taking the racket backwards in an arc. Remember, the closer you keep your right elbow to your body, the smaller the arc and the less powerful the swing will be.

Once the racket is swung above the level of your head, the racket wrist should be cocked and on contact with the ball it should snap forward to give that final power boost to your stroke from the combination of body weight, swing and speed of the racket head.

At the moment you make contact with the ball, your shoulders will have swung round until they are parallel with the net and on completion of the stroke you have turned from your initial serving stance and be facing towards the left-hand net post. Your body weight will have shifted forward automatically.

Always attempt to hit the ball at the very apex of the service toss, just as you should try to hit a forehand at the top of the bounce. That way you will ensure a better stroke and more power and accuracy.

This action is known as the flat serve, and is used by most players as their first service. If it should be a fault it is best not to attempt a flat second serve but to use a slice or spin.

The phrase 'flat serve' is not strictly accurate, by the way. Research has shown that, unless you are nine feet tall, you cannot possibly hit a truly *flat* serve which would get over the net and still land in your opponent's service box.

Figure 11 The service action and points to remember. (1) Weight on front foot. (2 & 3) Begin to shift weight backwards in preparation for the toss. (4 & 5) Throw the ball well up, arch the back and bring the weight forward. (6 & 7) Cock the wrist, bring shoulders square to the top of its travel. Let the weight continue coming forward and follow through fully.

1   2   3   4

So the ball has to be hit in an arc, allowing it to dip naturally over the net. And the danger with the straight, 'flat' serve is that in order to be effective it must be directed much closer to the top of the net than in the slice or spin serves.

This is not the case with the slice, which is well worth attempting to develop as your second serve because of its deceptive bounce and also because it will arrive on the opponent's racket with noticeably more speed than the ordinary 'safe' second serve used by so many people.

Delivered from the 'deuce court' (or right hand side of the court)

5   6   7

the slice serve will bounce away from a right-hander's forehand, pulling them out of court as they return the serve and setting up an easier second shot for the server. Delivered from the 'ad court' (or left hand side) it will swing into the left side of your opponent's body, or down their backhand side. And remember to keep these slice serves as deep as possible, rather than just floating them over the net. You must still try to pin your opponent back, because they are automatically looking for a short serve from which they can hit a winner.

On the slice the ball should be thrown up marginally farther to the

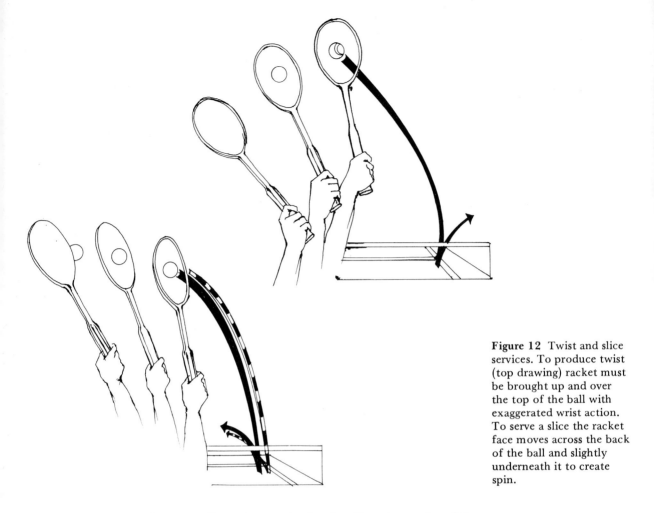

Figure 12 Twist and slice services. To produce twist (top drawing) racket must be brought up and over the top of the ball with exaggerated wrist action. To serve a slice the racket face moves across the back of the ball and slightly underneath it to create spin.

right than for the flat serve. In order to obtain the slice the angle of the racket face has to be changed so that at the top of the swing it will be moving across the back of the ball and on contact should be striking the right hand side of the ball and wrapping around it to create the spin which produces the slice. As in the normal flat serve, the racket continues to swing across the body and underneath the left arm.

Much more difficult to master is the twist serve, which demands more acute timing and wrist action than either the flat or slice serves.

The twist is something that it is better not to attempt to use until you have mastered the other two types of service. With its high, topspin arc and exaggerated bounce the twist invites a passing shot in return unless it is accurately placed.

Whatever type of serve you are planning to use, always remember to vary the angles, speed and direction as much as possible. Always try to keep your opponent guessing where you are going to serve. Sometimes it is a good strategy to aim the ball straight at them, not with the idea of hitting them of course, but by directing the ball down the middle of the box they can become confused, not knowing whether to play a fore-hand or backhand return.

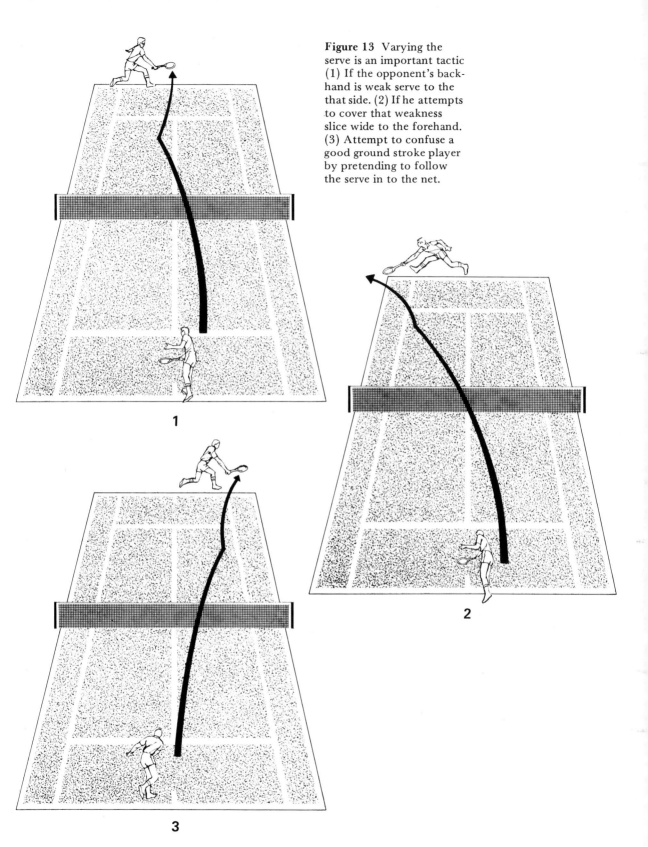

Figure 13 Varying the serve is an important tactic (1) If the opponent's backhand is weak serve to the that side. (2) If he attempts to cover that weakness slice wide to the forehand. (3) Attempt to confuse a good ground stroke player by pretending to follow the serve in to the net.

1

2

3

5. Returning Service

There are those who say that the serve is the most important stroke in the game. This being the case, the return of serve must be the next most important, since it is played on almost half the points in which you are involved in a match. Yet not nearly enough people regard it seriously enough to practise it with the regularity it deserves. The serve, yes. Forehand and backhand, of course. But return of serve seems to get relegated

far too often to the 'hit and hope' class.

There are so many options for you on the return of serve and if you have good, solid, dependable ground strokes it can be a very big shot for you. I know that I certainly rely a lot on my return of serve.

The first thing to bear in mind is that the return of serve as such is not a *specific* stroke. You can bring into play either your forehand or backhand, hoist a lob or loft back a little drop shot. Since the options open to you are so wide and varied, it goes without saying that the more planning and thought you put into the return of serve, the better the results will undoubtedly be.

It is most important, for instance, to know your opponent. Not socially, but as the person on the opposite side of the net. Compile a mental dossier on their likes and dislikes, how they throw up the ball, where they prefer to place their serves. At beginners' or club level it is very likely that you will know your opponent as a friend or acquaintance, but even if you have never met them before you can quickly establish all the above-mentioned factors.

The person who is serving is automatically on the offensive. The object must be to wrest that offensive advantage from them by positive thinking and positive action.

Figure 14 Returning service. Stand close to the baseline, balanced and alert. Try to return the ball from in front of the body to get better control. Watch the ball at all times until the stroke is completed.

Never, *never* hit your return of serve with no particular aim in mind. An impulsive swish, unless you are very lucky, will mean a poor return and that in turn invariably means a point lost. So plan your course of action.

Planning your return means that you must have your eye on the ball, and you must keep your eye on that ball, from the moment the server throws it up. Watching how and where the server tosses the ball will give you an early indication of which direction it ought to be heading and whether it is likely to be a flat, spun or sliced serve. For example, a lot of players tend to vary their toss a bit when they intend to serve wide, and this can be a useful forewarning. If the ball is suddenly thrown up a few inches further to the right than normal you can expect to receive a sliced serve and be prepared to move in that direction. Don't make

the mistake of watching the server rather than the ball. A lot of inexperienced players commit this rather elementary error. Never mind your opponent's wind-up, no matter how flamboyant, impressive or dodgy it may be. The ball is what you must give your undivided attention.

Where the server stands is also important. Most people take up their serving stance at the centre mark on the baseline, which is the shortest distance for a serve to cross the net. But beware those who may stand a little distance away from the centre mark in order to give their serves more angle or swing. A good example of this would be a left-hander standing well to the left on his own baseline and serving into your ad (or left hand) court. Assuming you were a right hander, his angled service could pull you sharply to the left, on your backhand — and almost certainly on the defensive.

Your own stance is the next thing we will deal with. Where to stand to receive service immeasurably increases your ability to return the ball positively.

You should position yourself on the baseline for the first service, and possibly a little behind the baseline if your opponent is a strong server. But never feel that it is a question of 'X marks the spot' for receiving service. Position yourself where you feel comfortably placed to deal with the serve, though you should never stand too far inside the baseline to receive a first serve, unless you know from previous experience that it is going to be a 'dolly' delivery (and in which case you should be thinking of playing somebody better!).

The general direction of your opponent's serve and your own returning strengths will determine how far over towards the sidelines you choose to stand. If, like most people, you are a right hander who is stronger on the forehand than backhand, you should position yourself nearer the baseline centre mark than the singles sideline when receiving in the deuce (or right hand) court, so that most serves will be directed at your strength. Adjust your position accordingly when facing a left-hander, particularly when receiving in the ad court as I have already mentioned.

Varying your receiving position, particularly if your opponent is holding service comfortably, could help to upset their rhythm or bring you a change of fortune. Try going a little deeper — but never so deep that you are obliged to return the ball from below the height of the net. Retreating a little like this might give your opponent more time to get up to the net but at the same time it allows you the opportunity to get right behind the ball and make a good, solid connection.

The question of running round a service also comes into this category. Speaking for myself, it's something I love doing. If you have a big shot and you are quick enough, then I would strongly advise it. I do it frequently in order to get the ball onto my forehand. If you do happen to possess a big shot it gets your opponent thinking 'Oh, I've got to get my return onto her backhand, otherwise I'm going to be in trouble'. This really puts the pressure on them, and when the pressure is on, the faults are bound to come as your opponent strives for the deep, far corners away from your strength.

However much you like to run around a serve in order to get it onto your strength, be careful not to overdo it, otherwise you'll find yourself dashing over into the next court in order to run round a serve which has been struck into your deepest backhand corner.

If the first serve is a fault, then you should prepare to move onto the offensive. Stand inside the baseline. This in itself is a slightly intimidating action as far as your opponent is concerned. It shows that you are prepared to attack.

To receive serve you should always be on your toes. Crouch down if you wish as your opponent goes into the service action, but once that ball is struck you should be up there on your toes ready to hit back. That's where skipping comes in, as far as I am concerned, as ideal training for quickening reactions. The very fact that you are on your toes will force your weight forward, thus avoiding the mistake made by so many people of receiving service in a defensive posture, the body weight back on the heels.

A good, controlled return is almost always made by hitting the ball well in front of the body. In order to hit the ball in front, particularly against a big server, it may be necessary to cut down on your backswing. So cut down the backswing if you need to, but never stint on the follow through. If you are moving forward, as you should be when you make contact, the abbreviated backswing won't matter.

Speed of reaction is so vital in returning serve successfully, and you must always take into account the type of surface on which you are playing your match. On clay, which gives a high bounce, you have more time to get into position and move that racket backwards. On faster courts there is much less time, so move more rapidly in making the backswing.

Finally, let's discuss what *type* of stroke you should attempt on the return of serve. If your opponent's first serve has been well delivered, you should get it out of your mind that you can hit a clean winner off it. This happens very rarely. Just make sure that you don't give your opponent an easy second shot. Against someone who stays on the baseline after serving, your best return is deep to their backhand, unless of course the backhand is your opponent's strongest wing. Aim for accuracy rather than pace in returning such a serve. The desire to hit a thunderous return is generally a rash one. By getting the ball back accurately and deep you have restored the rally to level terms in most cases. In women's play, where the girls tend to stay almost invariably around the baseline at club level, concentrate on feeding the ball back deep, breaking up the rhythm with an occasional short return to get her moving around more.

Against someone who is coming to the net behind their serve it is not really advisable, unless your standard of achievement is high, to attempt a passing shot. Return the ball as low as possible over the net, so that the shot will drop at their feet as they come charging in. Backhand or forehand, a low volley like this is not easy to play. They are usually forced to play the ball up, which neatly turns the tables and puts you on the offensive.

Against the second serve your options are much wider, unless the service is particularly well struck as regards depth, spin or slice. Here a drop shot can be an outright points winner, but a good, solid, thumping return deep to your opponent's baseline takes some beating — and takes some reaching too!

To sum up, attack a service, particularly a second serve, whenever it's feasible, but against a good serve your main aim should be to keep the ball in play. Force your opponent to play the ball a second time, then think about going over to the offensive.

6. The Forehand

The forehand is most people's strongest stroke, and in my case this is certainly so! The most important consideration is that it should be a natural shot. For instance, whereas most backhands tend to be very uniform, forehands differ a lot, and your forehand must come naturally to you.

Normally you can hit the ball a lot harder on the forehand side and, because it is a longer stroke than the backhand, you can get more speed

and power from it. Although you shouldn't consciously think of whacking it, the stroke has to be hit with authority. Not madly, but as though you mean it.

The forehand for most people is simplest of all to learn, and is in fact the basic stroke of the game. Holding the racket in the Eastern grip, your weight forward, body flexed and knees bent to react to the height of the bounce, you should always be prepared to move forward onto the ball, rather than let it come to you.

In other words, take the ball as early as possible, thus making sure that it goes back over the net an extra second faster to catch your opponent out of position.

Most forehands that go wrong do so at the very first moment, on the backswing. Concentrate on achieving a compact backswing, a rhythmic, circular motion, a flowing stroke, something that feels comfortable. Big looping backswings should be avoided at all costs. Windmill forehands like that totally lack timing and by the time you've hit the ball your opponent could have had a cup of tea.

The advantage of a compact swing is shown when you are running wide for a ball. It is much more advantageous to possess a shorter swing because with a big wind-up you would never have time to connect with the ball.

Figure 15 The forehand. Start the backswing early and make it as full as possible moving weight onto the left foot in preparation to hit the ball. Make contact in front of the body and, keeping your eye on the ball, make sure of a good follow through.

Beginners also make the mistake of starting their backswing too late, and not doing enough to co-ordinate swing, pivoting of the hips and proper footwork. As you begin the backswing the weight transfers from the front to rear foot and your body turns to the right, permitting the racket to be brought more easily into position. The racket should be drawn back so that it is approximately parallel to the body and between waist and knee height. Now you are in position to make the shot.

Shift your body weight from the back foot onto the front foot and move forward to meet the ball.

Every good shot is hit with the weight going forward. Even if you are forced onto the defensive and are running backwards for a shot you must always try to keep the weight as far forward as possible, because if you lean backwards the ball is automatically going to go up in the air.

The best practice exercise to ingrain this attitude is for someone to feed you with a succession of balls just in front of you, thus ensuring that you are always going forward. And remember, your attitude should always be positive. Go looking for the ball, don't let it come to you.

One of the most common errors in the forehand is in not giving the stroke enough follow through. Many players cut short the stroke as soon

Preparing to hit a forehand return. Watch the ball and give yourself room for a full backswing.

as they make contact with the ball, which then flies through the air with the greatest of ease and straight out of play!

I was firmly taught that the follow through is the most important part of the forehand. Like a golf swing you should feel that 'whoosh' when you hit the ball. A good exercise is to practise the follow through in front of a mirror until it feels completely natural and easy.

The follow through is also important for imparting more pace and power to your shot. I was taught to pull the racket right round over my left shoulder on the follow through, to exaggerate it almost, when I started to play. I cannot stress too heavily the importance of not 'quitting' on your shot at the moment your racket makes impact with the ball. Remember the good golfers, and swing right through your shot, just as they do.

Some coaching manuals talk about wrist action on contact with the ball, but I firmly believe that if you are just starting out to play tennis you shouldn't think of that sort of thing. If you start thinking consciously of hitting the ball with a firm wrist or snapping the wrist it will ruin your stroke completely. The wrist action is something that should happen naturally.

I am totally against people saying you should snap your wrists on contact with the ball. Every time I have tried to do that I just get a sort of flap at the shot rather than a true stroke.

The wrist is important, obviously, but if you are moving forward into the ball the wrist will automatically snap and give you that extra power. But if you cock the wrist consciously you will end up by exaggerating it and messing up the shot.

If you are not getting power into your forehand it is either because you have too big a swing or don't follow through. Don't try breaking your problem down into examination of the shoulders, elbows and wrists, because it will only worsen your troubles. Keep the swing basic, concentrate on hitting the ball firmly and things will automatically happen. Remember, you can't hit a forehand and follow through without your wrists snapping, so the thing to do is *relax*. If you are too tense when you make your shot things won't happen for you.

There are three types of forehand shot: the flat drive, topspin and underspin. I mainly hit flat forehands because I concentrate a lot on fitness and speed, which enables me to get to the ball a bit earlier than

Figure 16 The topspin forehand. Move early to the ball, racket face at an angle on the backswing. Move the racket through and over the top of the ball as contact is made, finishing in a high arc.

most people and therefore hit the ball at a higher part of its bounce.
I never ever let the ball drop below the top of its bounce, but always
hit it before it starts to drop. You get much more pace that way. So
if you're fit enough to get to the ball you can hit a flat forehand because the ball is bouncing so high, but the majority of my forehands
are hit with slight topspin to get better control.

It is when you are forced to take the ball low that you should try
a topspin return or a slice. The topspin, employed by so many professionals these days, causes the ball to rise higher than a normal flat forehand, drop sharply and bounce with a kick. To achieve topspin you do
not take the racket straight back, as in the normal forehand, but pull
it down below the level of the ball and create the topspin by the upward sweep of the racket on your shot and follow through. In applying topspin you are hitting a different part of the ball, the lower rather
than the central portion. Concentrate on achieving a circular motion
with the shot — back, up, over and round. But don't overemphasise
the swing, whatever happens. I'm not talking about windmills.

Slice, or underspin, is achieved by tilting the racket slightly back-

The running forehand.
Move quickly to the path
of the ball, hit it as soon as
possible after the bounce
and remember to get back
into position for the next
shot.

wards and coming down from over the top of the ball, hitting the back of the ball, then through the bottom of it, almost underneath. This puts "stop" on the ball and makes it float through the air more and bounce less when it lands. Personally, underspin is a shot I never use on my forehand, nor do many of the other top professionals. Its main usefulness is as an approach shot or a change of pace to break your opponent's rhythm.

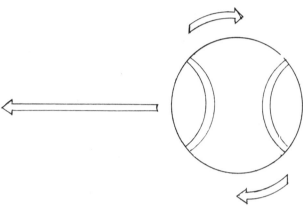

Figure 17 Imparting spin. Underspin is achieved by striking the ball below its centre line, helping it to 'float'. Topspin results from hitting over the top half of the ball, ensuring that it curves sharply downwards.

7. Backhand Shots

At club level the backhand is the defensive side, the weak shot of the average tennis player. It was true of me, too, at that stage and I still have to accept that my backhand is not my best side. So many people, quite naturally, want to have a super backhand but until you have literally practised for years this will not happen. In the meantime, use the stroke to the best of your ability and you will be surprised how much you can achieve in a positive fashion.

Never attempt to be too ambitious with the stroke, don't expect to do things that are beyond you while you are learning to perfect your backhand. It is a very difficult thing to obtain power from a backhand shot.

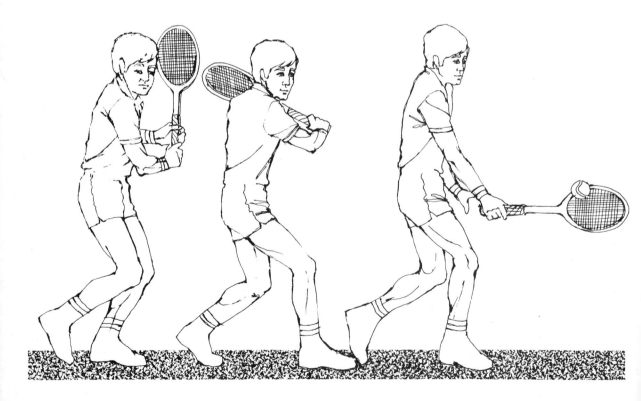

As far as I, and a good number of other people, are concerned, it feels a strange shot to hit because it is the sort of motion you never use in ordinary, everyday life. When I was learning tennis I certainly never felt relaxed or comfortable when I was executing the stroke.

For one thing, the backhand requires you to work on the 'wrong' side of your body and is carried out exclusively on that side in a series of movements in conflict with what we might term 'normal'. When you start practising the backhand, for instance, it will quickly become apparent that you are not built to hit it naturally. If the stroke *does* fall into place naturally, then you are the fortunate one in a million!

I can already see the question on readers' lips. Why is it that so many of the top professionals possess such marvellous backhands, better even than their forehands? Quite true, with a lot of tournament competitors it is their strongest stroke simply because it is a shot which demands so many hours of practice and perseverance.

As I have already said, you never *get* a shot properly until you have practised it for at least a year. And if you practise the backhand regularly every day, or as frequently as you are able, it can become your most potent shot.

Another great thing about the backhand stroke is that, once you become confident about playing it, you can do more with it than you can with the forehand in the matter of angles, touch, and that sort of thing.

Now let's deal with the basic execution of the backhand stroke. While

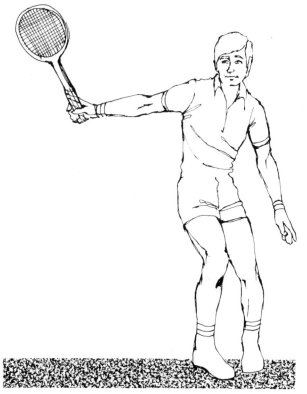

Figure 18 The backhand. Move towards the path of the ball as early as possible to give yourself plenty of room for a full swing. Shoulders should be fully turned, weight firmly on the right foot and knees flexed. Eye on the ball throughout and a full follow through.

I don't consider that footwork is as vital as most people stress in the backhand, it is obviously important in getting you into the correct position to deal with the shot. The first problem to overcome is that terrible feeling of 'Oh, no' when the ball is aimed down your backhand. Sooner or later you are going to face up to the inevitability of playing a backhand shot. So start learning how to do it properly!

As with everything else in tennis, try to keep the backhand simple. Like the forehand, you *must* hit through the ball with a flowing motion to achieve the results you are aiming for. Never prod, or poke at the shot. And remember, the backhand is easier to execute if you keep your body out of the way.

Early preparation to deal with a backhand shot is vital. Once you see the ball heading towards your left, turn your body sideways in that direction and your feet will move naturally into a position parallel with the baseline. As you prepare to play the shot keep your racket elbow close to your body.

Your anticipation and early preparation should have brought you into position to deal with the ball with a full, free arm-extended swing. Take the racket back, as with the forehand, in a circular motion, the head higher than the grip on the backswing.

As the racket reaches the top of the backswing, the effort of getting it into that position should have pulled your shoulders round into a three-quarter position towards the net, or in other words your back should be facing the right-hand net post.

By now your right foot should be well in front of the left, though not exaggeratedly so. Bring the racket forward at approximately waist height, pivoting your body naturally so that you are beginning to turn it once more towards the net. As you strike the ball your arm should be firm and the wrist locked and your weight moving, again, onto the front foot. The knees, of course, should be bent according to the height of the bounce to allow for this weight shift and also to permit any last-minute adjustment in body position.

The backhand. Wherever possible set oneself to play the balanced backhand but on occasions be prepared to move quickly from the baseline to deal with a short ball.

Figure 19 A good
example of giving yourself
plenty of room, taking the
ball early and comfortably.

As with the forehand, you should try to be moving forward as you strike the ball, though not to the same extent. Also, try to make contact with the ball while it is still in front of your body.

Now comes what I regard as one of the most critical parts of the backhand, the moment immediately after ball and racket connect. You have watched the ball right onto your racket (otherwise the chances of a faulty connection are high indeed). Now you must continue to follow the flight of the stroke, letting the natural follow-through swing of the body bring up your head.

On the follow-through the free (or left) arm should also fall into a natural counter-balancing position, roughly resembling a bird in flight. On the completion of the stroke your racket should finish, again as in the forehand shot, around shoulder or head height, depending on the spin or direction you have chosen to apply. You should be on your toes, almost square on to the net, well balanced, moving forward and thoroughly prepared for the next shot.

As I have already mentioned, most club players settle for the backhand as a defensive shot and nothing else, which is a shame. There are three types of backhand — the slice (or underspin) which is essentially defensive, the topspin, which is usually an attacking shot, and the normal flat backhand. The art of tennis is disguising what you intend to do. All backhands have the same take-back. It's what you do with the racket head on the follow-through that matters.

I say that the slice is essentially defensive, because you can often see Virginia Wade use a deep, sliced backhand as a good approach shot. To obtain slice you lengthen the circular loop on the stroke, bringing the racket back a little higher and swinging slightly *down* on the ball with a cutting motion as you hit through with your racket tilted marginally backwards in order to aid the underspin and to avoid propelling the ball low into the net with the downward swing.

Now let's get you into an attacking mood with the topspin backhand. Like every other backhand stroke it demands an awful lot of practice but the results are well worth it, since topspin can transform your whole thinking about the stroke.

To achieve topspin you need a lower-than-usual backswing and a high finish and follow-through. Though the ball is struck with the full, flat face of the racket the fact that the racket is moving upwards at the time of contact will impart the topspin needed to carry it safely over the net and land it safely within play on the other side. Since you are striking the ball with a flat racket face the stroke should be easier to learn than the slice, though the slice is a shot which comes more naturally to defensive-minded beginners. To achieve topspin there is one golden rule: the ball must be met with the racket on the rise.

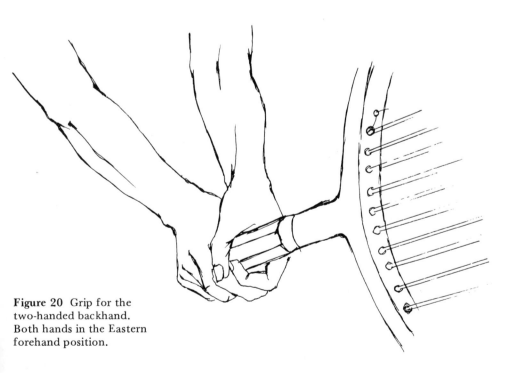

Figure 20 Grip for the two-handed backhand. Both hands in the Eastern forehand position.

No instructional chapter on backhands would be complete, of course, without reference to the double-handed shot. Though this is by no means a new, or modern, stroke it has gained enormously in popularity in recent years through being used by such stars as Chris Evert, Jimmy Connors, Bjorn Borg and Tracy Austin.

First of all, is it a good or bad stroke? That can be answered quite simply. If the four people I have just mentioned are happy using it, then it *has* to be a good shot!

But once again we must remember that we are talking in these pages about the beginner, or the average player who wants to do better. So let's discuss the pros and cons involved in the two-handed backhand at that level.

First, it's an easier stroke to teach to younger people who are not strong enough to generate strokes off a one-handed backhand grip.

Having been brought up with a one-handed backhand, I wouldn't recommend the two-handed method for older people who are taking up tennis. But for children who can't swing a full-size racket through, it is a very good way of learning. If this stroke develops into a good

Figure 21 The two-handed backhand stroke. As for the normal backhand ensure a full turn of the shoulders, weight on the right foot and a full follow through. Speed about court is essential to offset the extra step necessary to reach the ball.

backhand, then don't change it, for goodness sake. But if it doesn't feel comfortable, switch to one-handed when you are older and stronger. The transition is not a difficult one to make.

The double-hand backhand also enables you to generate more power and certainly more topspin, and it is easier to 'groove' your swing using both hands to control it. In the matter of topspin, I need do no more than remind you to look at Borg and see how exaggerated a topspin shot he produces from his backhand.

If it is a good shot from which to generate topspin, the double-fisted backhand is, by the same token, a stroke which does not make it easy to produce a slice. It also makes reaching high and low balls more difficult, but its main drawback is this: it is a little bit restricting if you are not particularly fast on your feet or quick in your reactions, because you have to take one extra step to reach the ball when you are running wide and if you are fully extended in this fashion there is less ability to achieve a full swing if you are clutching the racket in both hands.

When all this has been said, however, there is no doubt that it is an attractive looking shot and, in popular terms, a new one. It is also, of course, an imitative stroke because people have seen the top players use it. But I would find it rather too restricting myself.

But whether you choose to employ a one-handed or double-handed backhand, keep these points always firmly in your mind as you work towards making the shot so smooth and grooved that it becomes almost instinctive.

Take the ball on the rise whenever possible. That way you will return the ball across the net with more power than if you make the shot off a level or sinking ball.

Always, always, keep your eye on the ball, and never 'quit' on your shot, but follow through with a free, full swing.

8. Volleying

The volley is a stroke in which the ball is hit in full flight without first having touched the ground. Therefore the ball will be coming in your direction at a much faster rate, so the first requirement of the volley and the volleyer is fast reaction.

It is almost without question a vital ingredient of modern tennis, a shot that must be mastered by every player who wants to improve and

Figure 22 The volley. Knees flexed, weight forward and racket poised for either forehand or backhand volley. Only a short backswing and follow through are needed with the racket face kept slightly open to carry the ball over the net.

by every beginner who wants to advance along the correct route to success. There is, however, no doubt that beginners are afraid to play the volley, afraid to advance into the uncharted waters of mid-court and test the speed of their feet and their reflexes.

There is absolutely no need for that fear. Remember these obvious advantages: first, the shot is played from much nearer the net than when you hit a serve or ground stroke; second, the volley is a much shorter stroke and therefore easier to execute; and third, when properly played, the volley is bound to build your confidence, because it seldom misses.

Try to get it firmly fixed in your mind that volleying is fun. It is a stroke which can introduce much more variety and enjoyment into your game. I think young people enjoy volleying to a much greater extent these days. In that way tennis has changed a lot in the last five years.

People at ordinary and club level are volleying much more and using rackets with larger surfaces, like Pam Shriver does. I would really advise people to try going in to the net whenever they can sensibly do so. I am enjoying my own game much more over the past couple of years since I started volleying more frequently. It really *is* a lot more fun, and it also shortens the rallies, too, if you are a little bit tired!

Doubles is the best way of improving your volleying. In doubles you

The volley. Weight well forward, eye on the ball and make contact as early as possible.

simply *have* to learn to be a good volleyer, otherwise you won't be able to find a partner. And what you need to learn in order to volley well, in addition to the aforementioned quick reflexes and reactions, are the abilities to anticipate where your opponent is likely to return the ball, to watch the ball with even more hawk-like ferocity than on ground strokes, and to achieve good body balance through sound footwork.

Now the basics. First, the grip. It is advisable to use just one grip for both your forehand and backhand volleys, and the most adaptable is the Continental (see the chapter on racket grips). Among its other advantages stated in the section on grips it provides the best insurance against the racket twisting in your hand when the ball doesn't strike the exact centre of the strings. The Continental grip also slightly tilts, or opens, the face of the racket into the ideal position for volleying. There are those players who prefer to change their grips for the forehand and backhand volleys, but you have to be very quick with your hands to manage that. With the Continental, you can hit both sorts of volley without changing the grip.

The volley swing must be short and compact because of the need to strike the ball as quickly as possible. Hence the advice to punch the ball rather than swing at it. Always, even on low volleys, the racket head should be above the hand and the handle.

The racket should be held out in front of the body, you should be leaning forward, with knees bent, prepared to move forward. Make sure those knees are really supple, this is vital in volleying. Do not normally pull back the racket head farther than the shoulder on the backswing (anything more and the ball is likely to have whizzed past you).

Once you have got yourself into the right position on court, footwork is less important than other aspects of the volley. If your body is in the right place your feet will follow. The wrist should still be cocked as the racket is swung forward but should be firm at the moment of impact.

This point of impact should always, as far as is possible, be in front of the body, and the follow through should be short and compact. The reason for this is that, while you may be lost in admiration at your volley your opponent may not be quite so delighted, and you could find the ball speeding back in your direction a split second after you have dispatched it with such skilful ease. So you need to be ready for another volley, and then another if necessary before the point is won.

Although the correct advice is to punch the ball, with very little back-swing or follow through, it is important to point out that you need not try to slaughter the ball with your volleys. Placements collect more points than power. But *do* be positive. The volley is an attacking stroke, and this should never be forgotten. If somebody is hitting the ball towards you at a hundred miles an hour you should plan to feed off that pace with your volley. The racket and the stroke must be firm; you aren't holding a wand!

Don't volley blindly. You must have in mind where you intend to aim your stroke. The best volleys are deep ones, unless you are presented with a high return, in which case you can hit it downwards at an angle, but around and below the level of the net you should just concentrate on hitting the ball deep in the desired direction until you get the opening for a clean kill off a weaker return. In this respect you should always be prepared to hit two or three volleys before you get the right one to put away.

Figure 23 Backhand volley. Keep the wrist firm, the arm straight, weight well forward as you 'punch' through the ball with an abbreviated swing.

Figure 24 Playing all volleys off the front foot ensures solid contact and accurate placement.

I will explain a little further on this point, which is an important one. Unless someone who is playing the serve-volley game is really fast, they will be playing their first volley, from the opponent's return of serve, from just inside the service line. This means that the ball is almost certain to be below the height of the net and not sitting up to be put away for a winner. So your tactic should be to punch it deep to the most distant corner of your opponent's court rather than go for a winner off that first volley. Then you should really have the opposition at full stretch; this time the return is likely to be less tight, less difficult, and your chances of scoring a point from your next volley are immeasurably increased.

Of course, all this volleying business would be extremely pleasant and very simple if the ball always arrived at the point where you happened to be positioned. Unfortunately, opponents aren't always quite so considerate. The most popular way of discouraging volleyers from storming the net is to hit the ball past them as they come careering in. But all need not be lost for the fleet-footed and quick-thinking volleyer. Get your racket head moving forward and outwards as far and as quickly as possible, thus reducing the amount of ground you need to cover. Usually, when you have been pulled wide in this fashion your ability to hit a winner is considerably weakened. So open the face a little more to give the ball the lift it needs to clear the net and, if you are able, apply an 'open-faced hook' to your shot which will send it back over the net in the direction from which you have just come, thus wrong-footing your opponent.

More difficult to deal with than the wide passing shot can be the ball which is thumped straight at you. Apart from the sheer intimidating factor of seeing a shot screeching straight for your head or your midriff there is the need to be extremely quick in your reactions.

Should you be a little slow off the mark or lacking in positional sense you could find yourself having to learn in a hurry how to cope with lots of low volleys. The low volley is a nasty shot to have to play and the most important point to remember is, as Tony Trabert said in one tennis instruction book, 'recognise that you are in trouble'. The easiest place to hit a low volley is into the net, so take precautions. The most important is that you should *really* get down to this shot. Your knees must be flexed for normal volleying but they must be bent for the low volley, since you have to get right under the ball. Since the ball is well below the height of the net you in turn must hit it upwards in order to return it, and you can't do this if you aren't operating from a low position.

Don't try to be overambitious with a low volley. Tilt the racket face back a little more than normal to give you quick lift and clearance, and do your best to return the ball as deep as possible. Don't overdo the pace, however. This could bring disaster at the beginning or the end of the stroke, with the ball finishing either in the net or over the baseline.

You must also recognise the limitations imposed on your shot by the requirement to play a high backhand volley. Despite the complexity of the shot, try to keep the ball in view at all times as you move to it and try to play the shot in front of your body, as with other volleys, but remembering that the extra height enables you to hit down on the ball. Once more, avoid the impulse to hit a stunning winner and concentrate on returning the ball as deep as possible, preparing yourself quickly for the next volley and giving you more time to deal with your opponent's return.

What are the most common mistakes people make in attempting to volley? Standing too close to the net is one of them. Although it sometimes enables you to pull off a spectacularly-angled winner, you are extremely vulnerable to the lob. So try to position yourself a couple of feet inside the service line, at the junction of the two boxes to minimise the risk of exposing one side of the court too much and always looking for the chance to move forward.

Figure 25 High and low
volleys. On the high volley
a slightly longer follow
through helps to add
power to this attacking
shot. On low volleys
ensure that the knees are
bent and that racket hand
is level with racket head.

Another fault is not moving around enough at the net. Merely to be
standing there, flat-footed, is apparently enough for many players. Keep
on your toes, be poised to take off in either direction. There is also the
failure, even on the professional circuit, believe it or not, to get down
low enough to the low volleys.

To sum up in four words, 'short, sweet and simple' should be your
motto where the playing of volleys is concerned. Keep the swing compact
and connect as often as possible with the 'meat' of the racket to feed off
your opponent's pace.

HALF-VOLLEY

The half-volley is so called because it is a shot made almost immediately the ball bounces, virtually at ground level, and it is, to my mind, the most difficult shot in tennis. Timing is obviously important in all shots, but to pull off the half-volley you need absolutely perfect timing.

The half-volley is a shot that really should not be played very frequently. If you find yourself playing it, the reason is usually that you got caught out of position. You are immediately thrown on the defensive by the need to play a half-volley because you simply can't hit a winner off it unless your opponent is badly out of position.

It occurs most frequently in doubles play, and is a shot most people play when they are approaching the net and aren't fast enough to get to a volley. An excellent return of serve can also trap you into playing the ball from around your feet, the most difficult position, as you move towards the net after serving.

The most important thing about playing the half-volley is that, like the low volley, you must *really* bend your knees and get right down to the ball, even if it means almost touching the ground with your knees to do so.

Another similarity with the volley is that you should always try to hit the ball slightly in front of your body with your weight going forward. Again, you don't need a big swing, but you should employ more follow-through than the volley, enough to guide the ball in the required direction. Don't try to hit the half-volley too hard, just scoop it up with a natural motion and punch it as deep as possible into the opposing court.

The angle of the racket face is another crucial factor. The face should be open (tilted backwards) at all times because of the lowness of the shot, but the closer to the net you are the more open the racket face needs to be in order to clear the net.

One final tip. You must *always* be going forward to hit a half-volley. If you are moving backwards it means that you really should have hit a low volley.

9. The Smash

The smash, a stroke which 'puts away' an opponent's lob or high, weak return with a powerful overhead blow, is the most spectacular shot in tennis and one which also gives almost every player the greatest satisfaction. There's undeniably a feeling of 'take that, then' as you crunch away an overhead to terminate what might have been a long and tiring rally.

If properly struck, the smash gives your opponent less chance of getting the ball back than any other stroke. Therefore the smash must be classified as *potentially* a point-winning shot. I only qualify the statement because the overhead is a shot that must be made decisively, *but not over-ambitiously*. At the same time, however, you must not be tentative. The dividing line between those comments is just about as fine as the dividing line between a stunningly successful smash and one which is either dragged into the bottom of the net or mis-hit wildly out of play.

From this you will gather, quite rightly I might add, that the smash is one of the most difficult shots to master. The first thing you should organise is your condifence. To smash well you have *really* got to be confident. That's the big thing. You can't go up for a smash and be thinking to yourself 'Oh no, why did they have to lob me . . . ' I remember the days when I used to think that sort of thing. 'Oh, not a lob', I'd say as I scuttled back into position, and nine times out of ten I'd miss it because I wasn't thinking positively about it. So if you're not positive about smashes, don't hit them.

Sorry if I'm repeating myself, but once again it's a case of practice makes perfect if you want to develop a winning smash. Get out on court as often as possible, get some kind person to feed you lobs, and hit 20

The Smash. Follow the flight of the ball and help to ensure good balance by pointing the free hand towards the ball. Strike the shot at the top of the swing with the weight forward and follow through downwards.

Figure 26 The smash. Get into position as early as possible, follow the flight of the ball by tracing its path with your free hand, which also helps promote good balance. Take the racket in front of the body by the shortest route and not behind as in serving. Strike the ball downward and in front of the body at the highest point of the racket swing.

or 30 smashes until you actually look forward to playing the shot.

So confidence is the vital first ingredient. Don't worry if your pulse races and your stomach starts churning as you move under a particularly difficult lob. It's a feeling that has been shared in the past, and I'm sure will continue to be shared, by even the greatest players. But don't let your anxiety show, whatever happens. Your opponent should never be allowed to see that you dislike or fear the smash. There's nothing like a couple of smashes put away with a healthy wallop to boost your own confidence and dissuade your opponent from trying to lob you to death.

The actual hitting of a smash is like the serve in many respects, though in the case of the serve you can pre-determine the moment of impact, whereas the timing of the smash is dictated by your opponent's shot.

Once you see that tennis ball hoisted high into the air from the other side of the net you must immediately move into position to retaliate, and this usually means some quick back-pedalling, an awkward manoeuvre when it is considered that you must also keep your eye on the ball from the moment it leaves your opponent's racket. Bearing in mind that you should hit the ball from well in front of you — and further bearing in mind that you need to judge very exactly the descent arc of the ball — you need to be in position with as much time to spare as possible.

Before dealing with the racket arm, let's discuss briefly the important role of the free arm in the overhead shot. It is literally a balancing factor, for one thing, but much more besides. You may have noticed that a lot of top players (Tracy Austin is a good example) actually point at the ball with their left (or free) hand to line up their shot and also to ensure that they do not take their eyes off the ball for an instant. The free hand is sometimes very useful, too, for shielding your eyes from the glare of the sun.

Next you must bring your racket into the serving position behind your head by the shortest possible route. In other words, don't swing it round behind your body as you would do in winding up for the normal service action, but draw it up quickly in front of your body and let it fall behind your shoulder, at about head level, in what is sometimes known as the 'back-scratching' position. Imagine you are about to scrub your back with a brush and you'll get the idea.

Now you are in position, still watching that ball like a hawk, to hit the smash, which is, basically, a flat serve. Don't try to be clever by attempting to hit a sliced or spun smash. Accuracy and depth are what you should be aiming for initially, with the later addition — as you become more skilled — of power.

As in the serve, try to strike the ball at the highest point of the racket's swing, hit downwards and make sure your racket head moves through the ball. If you expose the ball to prolonged contact with the racket head you will 'drag' at the shot and send it into the bottom of the net. If the racket face is tilted backwards or if you strike the ball below the centre of the racket you are very likely to hit the ball deep and out of play. Until you are able to generate good pace from your smashes, try to get a little angle on the ball if possible. This will further ensure that if your opponent does get to the ball he won't be able to do anything positive.

The state of the weather is an important consideration in smashing. We have already discussed the blinding effect of the sun's glare. There could also be the problem of playing in a wind sufficiently strong to blow the ball about, and this is particularly true of the lob. In case you need to make a last-second alteration in your stance, always be on your toes ready to make that adjustment. Be prepared, it doesn't matter that you may have to wait what seems like hours for the ball to reach you, but you mustn't be just starting up your stroke when it is time to hit the ball.

In order to build gradually on confidence, it is sometimes a good idea to let a lob bounce before smashing it back, particularly if the lob, and the resultant bounce, are high ones. A strong wind is another reason for hitting lobs on the bounce on occasions.

Even hitting the ball on the bounce can be tricky, however. There is a tendency to stand too far back from the ball's point of impact on court, thus forcing the player to make a last-second, and usually fatally clumsy, adjustment in positioning. Remember that the ball will almost always bounce virtually straight up into the air, so stand close to the spot where you expect it to land.

If you should be caught out of position or off balance you may need to play what is called the leaping smash, in which you jump to meet the ball at a higher point. It goes without saying that your co-ordination needs to be even finer for this shot, since you are airborne at contact, than for the 'routine' smash. Your racket must be in the 'serving' position behind your head before you begin to achieve 'lift-off' with your right, or rear, leg. The leap and the swing must be a rhythmic combination, executed in harmony. Never jump and then start to swing the racket, or you'll make a complete hash of it. At the completion of your shot, as you swing forward and through the ball, you should land on your left foot.

If your opponent's lob is a particularly good one, or if you have been caught badly out of position, you may find yourself forced to play the backhand smash. This is a stroke, unlike the straightforward overhead, which can throw you very much on the defensive, because when you are hitting the ball backhand and over your head it is difficult to get any power into the shot. The best thing is to attempt to get it back deep or hit a short angle. Never put it straight back down the middle of the court. You will be 'dead' on your opponent's next shot. You are unlikely

Figure 27 The set up for the smash. The free hand, as well as giving balance, can also shade the eyes from glare.

to hit a winner off a backhand smash, unless you pull off a really good angled shot, so don't try. Just make your opponent's next stroke as difficult as possible.

Wherever possible, therefore, try to hit your overheads from the forehand side. Since you will normally have lots of time to get into position, you should be able to play the vast majority of your smashes in normal 'service' fashion. A final reminder that if you don't 'put away' the first smash, there's no need to worry. Your opponent will very probably be forced to lob again, and he's likely to make a poor lob before you miss a smash.

10. The Lob

The lob is popularly considered to be a defensive shot, even a boring shot. 'Childish' and 'cissy' are other descriptions which are regularly applied to the stroke. Not true, I'm afraid. Though I would agree that a match which consists of little more than lobs from both sides of the net (and I know this happens occasionally, usually at the most amateur of levels) is a boring sight, the lob is a vital part of your armoury, and this gentle, lofted stroke can prove a dangerous offensive shot.

A recent example of its effectiveness was in last winter's Wightman Cup tie at the Albert Hall in London. It couldn't have been more agonisingly poised — three matches each, the final doubles in its third and deciding set, Virginia Wade and myself leading Christ Evert and Pam Shriver 5-4. Pam was serving to keep the United States in the match. At 15-30 off her first volley I hit a lob which needed to be very accurate indeed to clear the impressive barrier of Pam's height surmounted by her large Prince racket. I knew when Pam groaned that the lob would sail too high for an attempted smash, and it dropped neatly into the corner of the American court. It couldn't have worked better, and it was a devastating blow for such a gentle stroke, taking Britain to match point. One rally later and the Wightman Cup was back in our hands. That's what I mean by a lob's offensive powers.

So don't hesitate to lob when you feel the situation requires it, either defensively or offensively. The top pros don't have any qualms about lobbing, so why should you? Forget any prejudice about the stroke being 'childish'. Use it for what it can so often be — a point winner.

Having said that let me add at once the important rule: Lob high, lob deep. Failure to do that will result in the game's horror shot, the short lob.

The lob has several useful advantages if properly employed. First, it can do a great job in breaking up an opponent's rhythm. For example, if you are playing someone who persists in coming to the net, a strategy which you are attempting to prevent by down-the-line passing shots, a lob thrown in occasionally is invaluable in helping to disrupt any rhythmic stuff from the other side of the net. By the same token it is also just the shot to drive back someone who persists in moving in right on top of the net.

If you have been drawn out of position by your opponent, the lob is

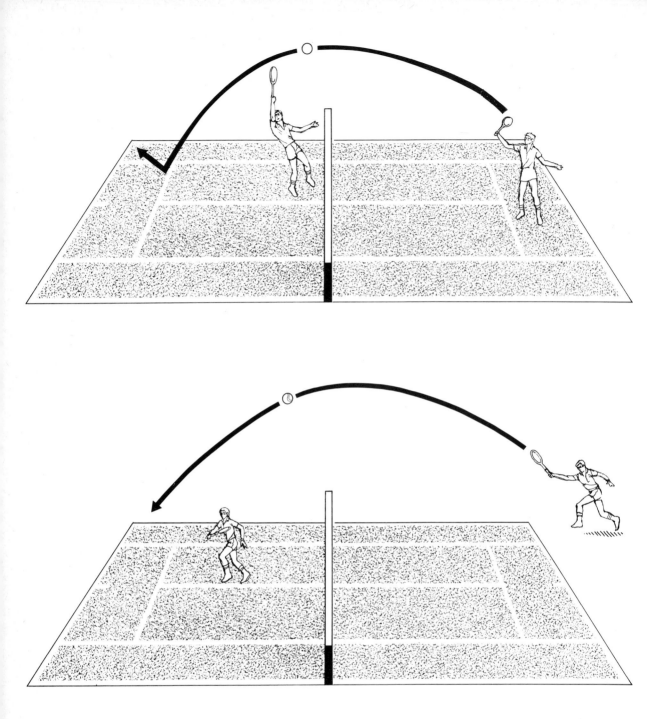

Figure 28 The lob. Both an offensive and defensive weapon. Used as an attacking shot it is normally hit quickly and low (but not too low) from inside the baseline. Defensively it is usually made from a deep position and hit as high as possible to allow time for recovery.

again most useful. Throwing up a lob gives you time to get back into position for the next shot. It can also, when properly executed, be a winner, demanding a superb smash from an opponent who is not capable of it.

The defensive lob is one which is most often played from deep behind the baseline or beyond the sidelines, where you have been driven by superior firepower or skill on that particular rally. This is when the lob, as I have said, provides you with a valuable breathing space and time to recover your poise and position and also robs your opponent of an easy winning volley.

The attacking lob is much more often struck from within the confines of the court, and is not hoisted so high as the defensive lob — but high enough to fly clear of an opposing smash, otherwise you have just played the horror shot, a short lob. This is a good tactic to use to keep net rushers at bay and shackle them to the baseline.

The same arm movement is used for both types of lob, and curiously enough you employ a more gentle shot to play the attacking lob. First, remember to hit through the ball, just as in groundstrokes, when lobbing. The difference is that you follow through with a long, smooth, rising motion of the arm to keep the ball in contact with the strings as long as possible. A vital point, this. So many people jab at their lobs, breaking up the follow through. The result: a short lob, and a point lost.

Remember again to disguise your intentions on the take-back and bring the racket head through below the height of the ball to emphasise the follow through. This is one of the few occasions when the racket head can properly be positioned lower than the racket handle. The shot can be made on either the forehand or backhand. As with groundstrokes, take the ball in front of and to one side of, the body to permit a fuller swing. The high point of your lob should be directly over your opponent's head, unless they are very close to the baseline of course, in which case you are not likely to be lobbing as a matter of choice, anyway.

On the offensive lob, tilt the racket backwards at less of an angle and cut down on the strength of shot so that the ball spends less time in the air and does not rise to the same height. Here again, however, failure to apply *enough* power could mean one of those disastrous short lobs.

You should make maximum use of court and weather when lobbing. Whenever you get the opportunity, try to lob diagonally, from corner to corner of the court. This will allow you more space to hit into and therefore less margin of error. Alternatively, lob down your opponent's backhand line.

The wind can be a valuable ally to lobbing. To throw up a lob into the wind is a pretty smart shot because it's always difficult to tell what is likely to happen and your opponent can't be certain by any means that a successful smash can be pulled off. Remember, too, that a wind blowing into your court will enable you to play the lob more strongly and with less predictability, while the same wind will slow down the speed of your passing shots.

The topspin lob is easily the most effective of the offensive lobs, but equally clearly it is the most difficult to master. The full range of ground strokes, including topspin forehand and backhand, need to be part of

Figure 29 When lobbing
avoid the fatal mistake of
hitting the ball with a
short swing. To get height,
length and control a full
follow through is needed.

your game before you attempt the topspin lob. Another point: it is a
more difficult shot for a woman to perfect than a man, because you
need a very strong wrist to hit the stroke properly. Martina Navratilova
is the best current example of a woman who can hit the topspin lob,
and when you look at the power in her left arm you know why. If you
still want to persevere in learning the stroke, here's how.

As with topspin serves and topspin ground strokes, the forward rotation
of the topspin lob causes the ball to be pulled downward more quickly
and to bounce much higher, two factors which immeasurably increase
an opponent's difficulty in producing an effective return. The topspin
lob is perfect for destroying an opponent stationed at the net; the ball
loops over his or her head, and bounces quickly away towards the back
of the court.

Because of the control required on this stroke, you need your footwork working well to get you into position to play the shot with the time
you need. From the backswing, bring the racket up underneath the flight
of the ball, making contact with the strings tilted only slightly backwards.

With your weight forward onto the right foot you should hit forward
and through the ball with an exaggerated upward swing. The wrist and
forearm action is all-important. The wrist, cocked on the backswing,

should be uncocked on impact with the ball, enabling the speed of the racket head to impart the topspin needed. The follow through should be long, high and as full as you can make it. Let the racket finish up well behind the left shoulder as you complete the great looping upward-and-over motion. Don't overdo the attempt at applying topspin initially.

The timing of this shot is so fine that you will get plenty of mis-hits as you work on it, even double hits as you try to apply the topspin while keeping the ball on the strings as long as possible. You will put the ball high out of court, low into the net and send back a few short lobs, too. But if you are able to persevere, a successful top spin lob is like a well hit smash, a most satisfying experience.

And for the majority who will employ the shot more conventially, always keep these points in mind. The lob is much more than a defensive stroke. When you employ it, lob high and lob deep and whenever possible, lob crosscourt. And turn a headwind into your lobbing ally.

11. Drop Shots

The drop shot is a stroke to be played, with occasionally devastating effect, against a slow opponent or to draw a baseliner towards the unfamiliar territory near the net. A lot of people use it against me, for instance, because of my preference for playing most of my tennis from the baseline, and they use it against Chris Evert, too, because they know she doesn't like to be at the net. I might add that Chris herself also plays the stroke very well. It will be seen at its most effective against an opponent who has been forced deep, or has chosen to stand deep, and doesn't

have the time or the speed to get to this dinky little shot. The surprise element is also considerable, so long as it is not over-used.

Having said that, let me follow up with a few warnings about when *not* to use the drop shot and how not to play it. It is a very ambitious shot, with little margin for error. The slightest miscalculation in making the stroke sees it either end in the net or turn into an easy short ball for your opponent. Therefore it is not the sort of shot for the average player to attempt on a crucial point, unless you are brave to the point of foolhardiness.

You may see a professional occasionally pull off a drop shot at a crisis point in his match, in an attempt to break up an opponent's rhythm, but people learning the game should realise that it is not a particularly high percentage shot for them. With more ability and a huge reserve of confidence you may eventually decide to try it on the big points.

I wouldn't advise you to use the drop shot against a weak second serve, either. There is much greater reward likely to be gained by returning

Figure 30 The drop shot. Mask your intentions by taking a full backswing as if planning a deep stroke. At the last moment, clip your racket gently under and through the ball with racket face angled backwards in a lifting motion. The follow through, though not as full as a ground stroke, should be aimed in the direction of the shot to ensure net clearance.

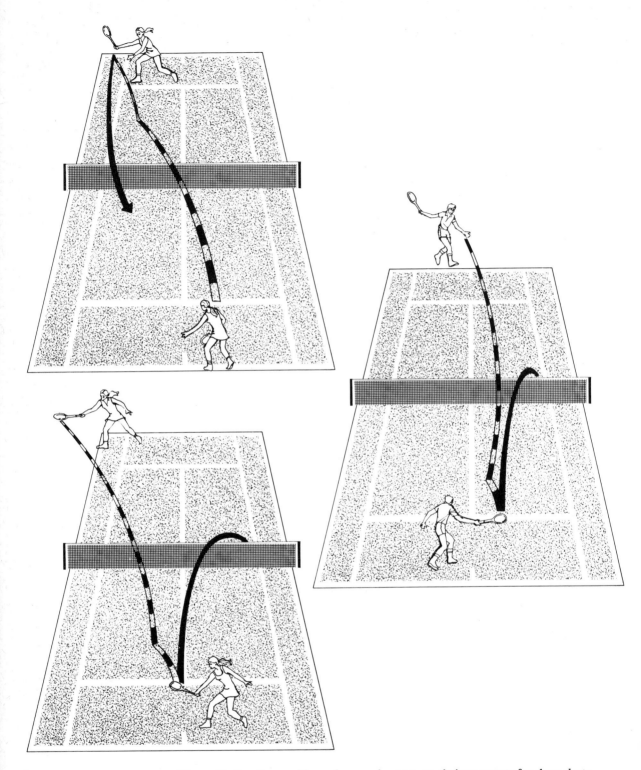

Figure 31 Baseliners with weak second serves are obvious targets for drop shots. Players who prefer to stay back can be caught out with a well placed shot and anyone who has been forced out of position and into a poor return can be beaten by this stroke.

such a serve hard and deep. It shouldn't be looked upon necessarily as a point-winning shot, but as a set-up for a winner on the next stroke. A common failing is that players tend to believe that the drop shot is going to be a winner every time. Not so. Always be ready for an opponent to get it back, though frequently all they can do, if it was a good drop shot, is to bloop it up for you to hit a winner.

The drop shot is, of course, one of the great 'touch' shots of tennis and developing this touch is certainly not acquired overnight. But be patient, don't be afraid to try it even if it costs you the point, and you will gradually get the hang of it. The time spent developing the shot will prove well worthwhile.

Masking your intentions is a vital ingredient of this shot, so that your opponent will be late starting for the ball. In other words, you take the same backswing for your forehand or backhand as if you were planning to hit a deep stroke, and then at the last moment clip your racket under and through the ball so that it loops over the net. In that way you will avoid sending a telegram to your opponent about your intentions.

This may not be quite as difficult as it sounds because your preliminary motions are the same as for a normal ground stroke. Never signal your plans by reducing the backswing; that should be as full as normal. The big difference only comes at the moment of impact. Tilt the racket face backwards, as for the lob, but continue to move it under the ball rather than upwards and through it. Try to keep the ball in contact with the strings as long as possible without actually catching it. Gentleness is the essence of this shot, so coax the ball away from your racket with a soft lifting motion.

The follow-through is not as full as for a normal ground stroke, of course, but it is a vital element of the shot nevertheless. The follow-through should be aimed in the direction in which you intend to make the ball fly. The follow-through, properly executed, ensures that your drop shot will clear the net safely.

Never hit a drop shot when you are standing still. You may have to slow down to make the shot, but never come to a complete stop because you may find yourself out of position if your opponent gets to the ball.

Your weight should also be forward. Just because you are playing a 'soft' stroke don't think you should be leaning backwards or holding back in any way.

Perhaps the most important piece of advice is that you should always aim to clear the net with your drop shot. If it plops into the net you have not only lost the point but lost it in an unnecessary and slightly foolish way by 'gifting' it to your opponent. So allow for good clearance, by feet rather than inches, and as your touch improves you will find that killable short balls become difficult drop shots.

The best direction for your drop shot is across court, because the angle will take your opponent even further out of court in a bid to reach and return the ball. You can sometimes set up the situation by hitting a forehand wide, forcing a return down the line, and following it up with a cross-court drop shot into the vacant spaces, which if properly played is guaranteed to make anyone run a very long way in a very short time. The ability to tire opponents in this manner by moving them forwards and backwards can be used to obvious effect.

Finally, bear in mind that the drop shot is a shot which wins points rather than matches. The percentage of failure or mistiming is too high for it to be otherwise. Retain it as a stroke which will continually surprise your opponent. Once alerted by over-employment of the drop shot, your opponent will turn the use of it to his own advantage. Only rarely can a good drop shot be returned for a winner, but by the same token only rarely does the drop shot itself provide an outright winner. Try to employ it, rather, as something which sets you up as the winner of the rally on the next stroke.

12. Techniques

THE BASELINE GAME

Most people play the baseline game by choice, since they feel more secure in doing so. Groundstrokes are safer than net sorties in their opinion, alternatively they may lack the mobility or confidence to get in to the net. If the baseline game is your most effective style, by all means play it. But to play it properly, you should be strong and as fit as possible.

The most important thing I was taught as a practice exercise was to concentrate on getting back into the middle of the baseline after every shot. Don't just stand there admiring your last lovely shot. It could be heading back in your direction with a bit of added venom in the next second or two. So get back into the middle as quickly as possible so that you don't leave a big gap on one side of the court for your opponent to hit into.

Patience is the greatest asset of a baseliner. The patience to wait for the right shot to attack, the patience to work an opening in a long rally, but initially the patience to groove your game into a rhythm and pattern by being willing to practise long and hard until your ground strokes are consistent. I know a lot of people find it boring, but you simply have to get out on court and drill, drill, drill. Hitting the same shot hundreds and even thousands of times is the only way to make it improve.

Only in this way will your game acquire the necessary accuracy and consistency — two ingredients which are absolutely vital for the successful baseline player. Only when you have achieved accuracy and consistency should you then employ the groundstrokes, and especially the forehand, for what they are essentially designed to be — attacking strokes. There is nothing calculated to make you more downhearted than to lose the point on an error committed unnecessarily while attempting to take the offensive.

So in your practice sessions, and in your matches too, concentrate on getting a length on your ground strokes, otherwise you are going to have people barging up to the net and ending the rally in rather violent fashion! At practice, be repetitive, hitting shot after shot up the line or across court and aim for a particular spot deep in the other court. You can mark the spot with some small object such as a racket cover, or better still just memorise the area you're aiming for — in that way you will prepare yourself more readily for actual match conditions.

Play the ball deep and give it a good net clearance, which will bring you the required length of shot without excessive effort. You can save those powerfully struck net-skimmers for the more advanced stages of your game. Returning a ball that's waist-high or net-high at the moment you hit it, you can afford — against an opponent who is also staying back or who has been forced back — to give yourself a safety margin of from two to four feet net clearance on your stroke, especially if you are applying top spin. But beware of putting up an easy shot for a net rusher.

The use of width in your ground strokes is another important consideration, keeping your opponent off balance and running hard. But here again you should allow yourself a comfortable safety margin, something like two-feet inside the sidelines and perhaps a yard outside the baseline. And as your proficiency improves you can start cutting the margin a little finer.

When you are facing another baseliner who is beating you with a better brand of consistency it is important to attempt to break up their rhythm by changing the pace on the ball. Loop one up, then hit the next one hard, it's surprising how many baseliners get themselves not so much into a groove as into a rut and are upset by a simple change of pace like that. For a comparison I could perhaps say that it's a bit like the difference between me playing Chris Evert and Betty Stove.

When I play Chris we tend to have a tremendous number of 20-shot rallies as we both work our way for an opening, but against Betty you simply don't know what's going to happen. You never get two shots the same, so you are never able to settle into any sort of rhythm.

Make your opponent think. Another good way to break up rhythm is to play a short angled shot, or a drop shot. Either of these, if properly executed, will bring your opponent scampering off the baseline and provide a test of quickness and stamina.

Never rally aimlessly, without any sort of game plan. Tennis is like a chess game, you have to manoeuvre your opponent around the court and then trap him. Watching a tennis match from a good height shows this up very clearly. You can plot where the players are likely to hit the ball and what they're concentrating on. You can generally guarantee that the top players are hitting good, deep ground strokes until they get the opportunity to do something better.

Another 'don't': never play a 'nothing' shot, hoping that your opponent will mis-hit it. That is the very reverse of positive thinking. But by the same token don't try to do too much, especially on an unsuitable ball. So many people try to hit a winner off a short ball played into mid-court. There is a tendency to rush this shot in a bid to put it away, which can lead to all sorts of disasters. Be patient. Wait for the right shot. Return that short ball deep and get yourself set to make a winner off the next stroke, or the next one after that.

Now let's deal with the method of counter-attacking an opponent who keeps on coming in to volley. The first thing to bear in mind is that, unless they are very quick on their feet, they will have to play their first volley off your service return somewhere around the service line.

The best tactic is to hit the ball back, dipping over the net towards the feet of the would-be volleyer. This will force them to play a low volley and unless your opponent is a very good volleyer indeed you will be getting a shot in return off which you can do something positive. A difficult volley like this is much better than an attempted big shot. Don't be tempted to try to hit a winner off their first serve or approach shot. Unforced errors are a good deal less of a problem for your opponent even than comfortable volleys.

Although patience is undoubtedly a virtue among baseliners it is important always to be thinking in terms of 'offence' rather than 'defence' in rallies, even on your backhand. It is wrong to attempt simply to keep the ball in play from your backhand, hoping that eventually the opportunity will arise for you to get round to your forehand. But don't be afraid to run round onto your forehand, if it is your stronger side, in order to thump a heavier return.

To sum up then, a baseliner should be fit enough to run for a long time without wilting, should always aim to get back to the middle of the baseline as quickly as possible after making a shot, and should possess patience, consistence and variety of shot. With all that, it's easy!

THE NET GAME

The first thing that nearly all beginners, and a good number of more experienced players, need to overcome in net play is a fear of going up to the net. This fear is usually a mixture of being afraid of being hit by the ball and being made to look a fool by going up on the wrong sort of shot.

Fears of being hit by the ball are usually quite groundless, although understandable until that fear is overcome. The first thing to bear in mind is that you could probably stand at the net and catch most of the balls that are aimed in your direction quite comfortably. So if you can catch it, it goes without saying that you ought to be able to hit it.

Get a friend to hit a few balls hard in your direction as you stand at the net. To begin with, just let them bounce off your racket — and you will be surprised to see how fast and far they *do* bounce sometimes. Then start taking a short swing at the ball. Remember the volleying swing is much shorter and simpler than a ground stroke.

As for the fear of being made to look silly, well you just have to learn from experience which balls not to move in on. You are bound to be passed from time to time, however good your approach shot, so don't let it bother you and inhibit you from getting up to the net.

Never to go up to the net is to impose a crippling restriction on your game, rather like people who play golf all their life with a quarter-swing. You'll never get beyond a certain standard, and you'll certainly get beaten by more adventurous and positive players. Moving up to play a short ball and then turning round to get back to the baseline is not only poor strategy but it releases your opponent from problems of pressure. Furthermore, the sight of someone moving in towards the net behind a good approach shot tends to induce uneasiness or even panic in some opponents. And conversely, the feel of a sweetly hit volley is a wonderful confidence booster.

Now let's move on to *when* and *how* to come in to the net. You can come in to the net with plenty of confidence behind a good first serve. The best time to attack the net off an opponent's shot is to pounce on a short or high ball or a weak second serve.

Getting on top of a 'soft' second serve gives you a great chance to get into volleying position, and is an excellent way of making the server nervous as they prepare to serve and see you moving forward ready to 'kill' the ball. Often they think to themselves 'Oh dear, if I don't get a good second serve in, she's going to be right on top of the net.' And this sort of thinking is so often the prelude to an abysmal double fault.

If you are playing someone whose whole game is a steady one, the second serve is probably the best time to attack, preferably with a sliced shot because it tends to keep much lower. A sliced approach is a better one to use than a top spin in this case, because your opponent will have to dig the ball out and, with a bit of luck, give you a nice high volley to move in on. People don't usually hit winners from around their ankles, so the lower you keep your approach shots the more chance you will have of an easy upward return that can be put away.

Now the question of how you move in for the volley. First rule: never, never rush the net; don't sprint. You must be quick, that goes without saying, but never move forward at the expense of balance and smoothness. If you are off balance all is lost.

The idea in getting up to the net is to make yourself difficult to pass, so positional sense is important, too. If your first volley, which should be made from around the service line, is a good, angled one you can feel confident about moving right on top of the net for your opponent's return, knowing that he will be too extended to do much more than spoon it back at you.

But if you move on top of the net against a prepared opponent you are risking a lob. Many club players persist in standing right up to the net and pay the penalty of being lobbed until they run themselves into the ground. It's a question of studying closely the person you're playing. If it's someone who doesn't have a good lob you can get away with coming right into the net, but if you get caught twice you must retreat because you know then that your opponent has uncovered a weakness in your technique. Keep that in mind always: if you miss one shot twice, then you must change your thinking about it and your manner of dealing with it. I know that if I was lobbed twice I would certainly stand back a few feet.

Not *too* far, mind you. That's almost as bad as being too close in. If you are too far back you will find yourself stretching for low volleys, and as I've said there aren't too many winners hit from around the ankles. If you tend to hang back, try to realise that the net game is based on attack, not defence. When you come in you want to be hitting down on the ball, above the height of the net, to build your point-winning position.

I stress the word 'build' because rallies aren't always won with a first volley. If, as is likely, you are volleying from about halfway between baseline and net, even a deep, well-placed shot won't beat a prepared opponent. So keep that first volley within the bounds of safety and sanity. Concentrate on getting into position for your opponent's return and your own second volley. If it is played properly, this sequence will win the point for you far more often than not.

A keen sense of anticipation is invaluable to the volleyer. In top women's tennis both Evonne Goolagong and Martina Navratilova have terrific anticipation. They can be in the middle of the court and you have the choice of trying to pass them on either side, but they always seem to go the right way when you make your move. One tip is to watch the movements of your opponent's racket head for clues.

This ability to 'read' an opponent's mind and intentions can win many points, and there's no magic involved in the technique even though you may sometimes get that impression when someone is anticipating your best shots.

Your sense of positioning must be very acute, and this only comes with experience unless you are particularly gifted. Once in position be poised on the balls of your feet, leaning forward. Don't bounce up and down. That's quite stupid in that particular context. So is swaying from side to side. You may be swaying in one direction when your opponent hits the ball past you in the other. If you so desire, you can leave one side of the court marginally more open for the return, inviting your opponent to play it, for example, onto your stronger volleying side.

13. Tactics

Tennis is a battle of minds, just as much as it is a battle of playing ability. Trying to expose your opponent's weakness is one of the most vital and fascinating facets of tennis. I have dealt with the mental side of the game in a separate chapter, but I can't stress too strongly the need to think your way through a match. Don't relax your mind any more than you

would relax your body. The penalty is the same — defeat.

If you know your opponent's weak points from previous experience, play on them — but be careful not to overdo it. If you haven't faced your opponent previously, try to uncover the weak parts of their game. Careful observation should quickly reveal them.

Always think what you are going to do to your opponent, not what they are going to do to you. For instance, if you are a baseliner and even if you don't have a big shot you can still move your opponent around with accurate placement and variations of pace and length. This is where fitness comes in. If you are the fitter person and you have just won or lost a long rally and are feeling pretty shattered just imagine how the person across the net must be feeling! So act on it. Think to yourself, 'Right, I'm going to make them run till they drop'. That is when playing a pattern of points is useful in winning rallies.

Against a few of the players I have faced I have thought, 'For the first four games I am just going to run from one side to the other. I don't care if I'm 4-0 down but after those four games they will really know they have been working hard. Then I'll know if they're fit or not'. The reverse thinking applies, of course, when someone who plays a similar sort of

Some fine examples of the power that goes into one of the strongest forehands in women's tennis. Aggression and determination are the keynotes.

game to your own has to be worn down by a pattern of shots, one corner to the other, for half a dozen games if necessary.

While you need to play a pattern of strokes for the rally, you should be very conscious of only playing one *point* at a time. Concentrating only on the stroke you are playing is all very well, but having in mind what your next shot ought to be does not lessen your chances of playing the current one successfully. You need to be thinking of your opponent's likely direction and strength of return and of your own next position and stroke. But it is often fatal — and distracting — to start thinking ahead to what *might* be if you win the next two points.

For instance, in love-40 situations you obviously have to play one point at a time. Just think to yourself 'If I can win this game from love-40 down it would destroy my opponent's confidence'. I know that if I ever lose a game from 40-love up I'm just so mad. And if you get that sort of feeling you know that's how they are going to be feeling, too.

Although it goes without saying that you should try to win every point, it is also clearly true that in tennis some points are more vital than others. These we call the 'pressure points', like 40-30 or 30-40, Ad-in or Ad-out. Thirty-all is also a crucial stage of any game. This is when you've *got* to win the next point, to bear down. If you've got a big shot, move your opponent round until they give you the shot that you want. Alternatively, save that moment to attack their weakness. The pressure point is the one that you have to apply everything to. Give it one hundred and one per cent.

One final thought about 'percentage tennis' and the points involved: you could win 14 games to your opponent's 12 and still lose the match 4-6 6-0 4-6. So remember those 'pressure' points and make your best tennis count at the right time.

On the question of games, we hear a lot about the 'vital seventh' game in every set. So many people regard it as the pivot point of a set. True, in a normal-length set, such as 6-4, it can be a critical stage. But the seventh game of the match could in fact be the first game of the second set if you're doing well — or extremely badly! I don't agree with the 'vital seventh'. To me every game is vital, and the first game of the match is the most vital, because it can get you off to a good start.

Let's deal next with that question of getting off to a good start, and whether you should elect to serve or receive if you win the spin of the racket. I usually elect to serve unless I am opposing someone with a big service. Then I like to let them serve first because they are serving from cold and you are more likely to get a break in those circumstances. Against a big server it usually works out that you have a better chance of a break in that very first game; they may not be mentally into the match, either. Someone like me, whose return of serve is their best shot, can snatch a vital early advantage in a match by these tactics.

A good tactical point to keep in mind on your own serve is to hit the ball directly at your opponent, especially if they are being a little cheeky or over-adventurous by standing up rather close in the receiving position. Serving the ball at them means you aren't giving an angle for the return of service, and not giving them much time either to fend off the shot which is homing in on their midriff. Generally you will get a return straight down the middle from this type of serve, enabling you to dominate the rally.

When serving you have the same advantage that a fast bowler ought to enjoy over a batsman by being able to keep your opponent off balance with a variety of deliveries: a fast, flat serve followed by a ball sliced away to the backhand side, followed by a high kicking delivery, and then perhaps a taste of 'body line' to add to the uncertainty. Whatever you do, never adopt a 'serve and hope' attitude, contenting yourself with getting the first serve into court and hoping that a mistake will come from the other side of the net. On the serve the advantage should be yours. Seize it.

This holds good on the second serve, too. We have already discussed in another chapter the perils of putting over a 'patsy' second serve. Try to put enough pace or cunning into it to ensure that you are not immediately forced onto the defensive. The hours spent developing a worthwhile second serve are rewarded in more ways than one. First, it relieves you of the worry of putting everything into your first serve, and second, your opponent won't be heaving a sigh of relief if your first serve is a fault.

Since the great majority of tennis in Britain is played outdoors the weather is obviously a very important element and one which you can use to your advantage. Not many matches take place in dazzling sunshine or a howling gale, but the sun and wind are important considerations. Don't let yourself be put off by what you consider is an adverse weather factor. Remember that it's the same for your opponent.

If, for instance, you find that you are serving first into a bright sun, don't appear obviously upset by this handicap by shuffling into different, wider serving positions and muttering about it. Use the warm-up period to assess the sun's angle and what you must do to overcome it. Don't throw the ball up directly into the sun or you will still be blinking and peering over the net when your opponent's return whizzes past you. Keep your throw as normal as possible, but just beyond the glare of the sun, and move a little wider in your baseline position if it takes you out of the sun's line.

In the wind, depending entirely on which way it is blowing, your margin for error or your safety cushion must be varied. On a deep shot the wind can move the ball a foot or so. On a crosscourt wind, therefore, you should aim your shot three feet inside the sideline instead of two.

But the same crosscourt wind can be a blessing. For instance, against someone who is coming up to the net a lot you can afford to hit your passing shots a little wider down the line knowing that the wind will blow them back into court.

Playing directly into the wind should never be something about which you allow yourself to get upset. A head wind permits you an excellent safety margin for your ground strokes, and especially for your lobs. Against the wind you can really lob with confidence, knowing that the ball will not only be held back but will move about in the air as it descends, giving your opponent a tricky smash if the lob happens to be short.

When serving into the wind, remember to throw the ball a fraction farther forward on the toss. Concentrate on getting as much speed as

The golden rule of tennis: keep your eye on the ball at all times.

94

possible into the serve, with good net clearance, and let the wind do the rest rather than attempting to put spin or slice on the ball.

With the wind at your back, good control is your first requirement. That, and a decent safety margin to compensate for the extra length the wind will impart to your shots. On the serve, your toss-up should be a shade further back. Don't find yourself straining to reach and hit a ball that is already floating away from you. If that happens, catch the ball, apologise to your opponent, and go into your serving action again. But don't do that sort of thing too frequently, or there could be murmurs of gamesmanship levelled against you.

Properly harnessed, a following wind can blow you to victory by adding speed and depth to your accuracy and control. It can be a formidable combination as long as you keep your head and don't become over-ambitious.

Like the sun and wind, the surface on which you are playing has a tremendous influence on the way the game is played. Grass and wood are very fast surfaces, with the ball keeping low and 'skidding'. Cement, too, is a fast surface, though it gives a friendlier, higher bounce, while on clay or composition courts the ball sits up and gives you more time to make your stroke.

Clay's yielding surface, and also grass, enable the player to slide into a shot, a style favoured by many of the Continental players. Indoor surfaces, whether wood or carpet, do not permit this, which is why some professionals initially find it difficult to adjust when they make the switch from outdoors to indoors.

Indoors, too, you can expect the conditions to be consistent. There's no sun or wind to contend with, but indoor tennis can provide its own particular dazzle problem with the lights, particularly if it is direct lighting. So here again you may find yourself having to slightly change or modify your service stance or throw-up to accommodate this.

The unavoidable confines of an indoor court can also cause problems when you are lobbing. Remember that the ceiling height may be limited, or that light fixtures or girders might get in the way. It is particularly frustrating to lose a point on what otherwise would have been a winning lob because of overhead obstructions. So tailor your lobs to the height of the ceiling and the ironwork, or if the roof is a particularly low one, cut the lob from your tactics on that occasion.

Finally, what sort of tactics should you adopt on one of those days when nothing will go right for you?

One of the oldest sayings in tennis is that you should always change a losing game. True, but first you might perhaps examine *why* you are losing. If you have had a spectacular run of bad bounces, net cords and other ill-luck, you ought to press on with your normal game in the knowledge that, hopefully sooner rather than later, your fortunes will change for the better. It's certainly no good appealing to the heavens, sulking, slamming the ball wildly out of court or throwing the match away. If you are simply being outgunned and generally outplayed it could be worth examining what's wrong. If you think you are feeding your opponent's strengths, try to vary your game. Break up your opponent's rhythm. If you are getting nowhere on the baseline, try coming in now and again. If your aggression is being turned against you, switch to a more subtle approach with the help of drop shots, lobs and sliced returns.

But face up to the fact that, on some days, your feet don't appear to have any relationship to your legs, nor your hands to your arms. If you are playing badly and nothing will change it, accept it as gracefully as possible, and attempt to salvage something from the grim occasion by noting your opponent's strengths and tactics. Then tell yourself that the next time you meet it will be different!

14. Doubles Play

Doubles is the backbone of the game of tennis. Partly because of the shortage of court space but mainly because of its social aspects, doubles is the popular game at club level. It is more sociable than singles, less tiring for most people and provides the same basis for keen but friendly competition as golf's weekend foursome.

Doubles is endlessly fascinating, with its patterns and possibilities, and it is no exaggeration to say that it is literally a different game from singles. To start with a rather obvious but important comment, it involves four players rather than two, and while this undoubtedly cuts down on the amount of running around you need to indulge in, it multiplies the amount of strategy, tactics and mental activity involved. In other words you always have to be thinking about your partner.

First, let's get rid of any misconceptions about doubles being a version of tennis for those who are too slow or old to play singles any more. While undoubtedly doubles is enjoyed by older club members, it is indisputable that it offers enough pace, power and tactical variations to keep all but the most dedicated singles fanatic contented. Having said that, I must add that in doubles it's a case of having to play smarter rather than harder if you want to make your game better.

In doubles there is more court to move around in, but less space to hit into — and also less to defend — than in singles. The 4½ foot wide doubles alleys running down each side of the court add another 700 square feet to the court area, but the presence of two people on the other side of the net places a premium on accuracy and 'touch'. It is placement rather than power that tends to win the points in doubles. An opponent standing at the net can feed off your power; make him stretch and reach for softer, angled shots.

You only have to cover half the court. So power, although it is a good thing to have, isn't all-important. The opposition can cover both wings of their court, or should be able to, so it's not likely that you will be able to strike a clean passing shot past them. That sort of shot comes off about one in ten in doubles. In this version of tennis the emphasis is on angles and placement and dependability. Wood shots and other mis-hits, the sort of thing that can frequently mean a winner in singles, are invariably heavily punished in doubles, where there will be somebody stationed at the net to put them away.

You will never achieve much in doubles until you digest the basic fact that you are not playing for yourself, but as a team; not trying to strike a spectacular winner necessarily, but attempting to set up a rally which can be won by your partner too. An excellent sense of communication, understanding and balance will go a long way towards making two people a formidable doubles team, no matter what their ability.

When I was younger and learning my tennis under Arthur Roberts at Torquay, I sometimes used to say to him, 'Let's have a doubles'. Mr. Roberts would invariably reply, 'Alright, but first we'll spend 15 minutes talking about it'. And I feel that's the reason why I won more doubles tournaments as a junior than any other British girl.

Tennis is more fun when you are able to talk about it while you're playing. You get the feeling of doing something more constructive by discussing tactics and problems, and you can also learn a lot from your partner.

So often you will hear people say, 'We didn't play well because it was our first match together. We just didn't have any understanding'. My reply to that is that it only takes five minutes before a match to discuss tactics and, as I have just pointed out, there is plenty of opportunity during play to communicate.

The first time Ann Kiyomura and I played together we won a big tournament in Japan because we struck up a quick understanding. It doesn't always work that well, of course. Normally the longer you have played together the better team work you will have, the smoother your movements around the court, the more positive your shot making.

For instance, a consistently accurate first serve reduces any potential danger to your partner at the net and also increases the chances of striking a winner off a weak service return. Good doubles combinations know instinctively which one should go for a ball down the middle, when both should advance to the net or both pull back to the baseline.

Although you don't have to be bosom friends, harmony is essential. For years Bob Hewitt and Frew McMillan have been a formidable combination because they have harmony on court. They have the quality of complementing, rather than duplicating, each other's skills. This sort of balance will mean that a team of average players usually ends up beating an opposing pair consisting of one very good and one not-so-good player.

I suppose, as Frew says, it's a bit like a marriage really. You cherish your partner, help them out in times of trouble and look with confidence for assistance when you're in a spot of bother yourself. It's certainly true that nobody ever won a doubles match by himself or herself.

Now I want to break down the doubles game into two sections, the technique and the tactics.

TECHNIQUES

In this section I will cover each of the main strokes as it applies to doubles, how it should be adapted and augmented for the four-person game rather than singles.

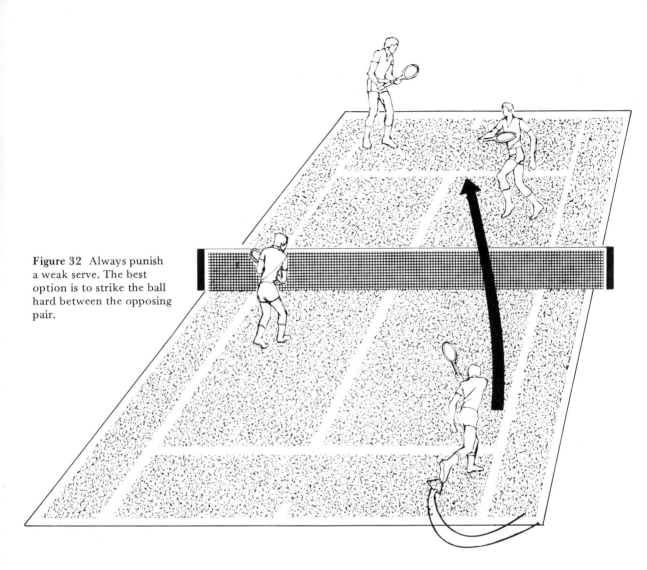

Figure 32 Always punish a weak serve. The best option is to strike the ball hard between the opposing pair.

First, the basic differences: your serve needs to be consistent, based on accuracy rather than power, in order to help and protect your partner stationed at the net. Your return of serve, too, needs to be consistent. Don't, in normal circumstances, go for an outright winner unless you are moving in to pummel a weak second serve. And, most important of all, good volleying ability is essential. You won't get away as easily in doubles with being a baseliner as you might be able to in singles.

Speed off the mark is more important in doubles because there is less time and space in which to operate. You must move in quickly behind a good first serve to get into the volleying position for instance and join your partner in an attacking position at the net. Allied to speed must be the same positive attitude that you ought to take into a singles match — move forward to meet the ball as often as possible. Also, it's even more important to make the conscious effort to keep your eye on the ball at all times, since it is flying backwards and forwards at a much faster rate than in singles and there are more chances of being distracted.

Although, as I have pointed out, accuracy is more important than sheer power in doubles, your shots still need to be aimed with as aggresive an intention as possible. Defensive thinking leads to tentative tennis, which in turn leads to lost matches.

Get up to the net as frequently as possible. That's where the doubles game is dominated from — and therefore won from. If your volleying ability is poor, remember that it will never get any better by avoiding the volley. The only way to improve is in the heat of battle, and once your volley becomes more potent it automatically makes your service less likely to be a liability.

Whereas in singles you should take up your service stance as close as possible to the baseline centre line, in doubles play your position should be about midway between the centre line and the outside of the doubles 'tramline', or even further towards the side of the court if you are seeking an even wider angle for your serve, and attempting to pull your receiving opponent right out of court. Serving from this wide position also enables you to move quickly into your 'half' of the court and be in position for the service return.

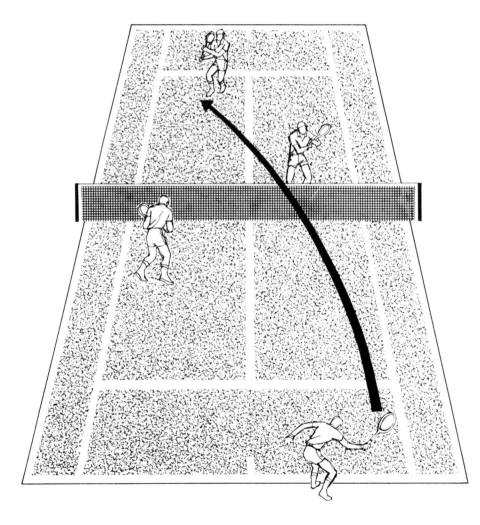

Figure 33 Returning serve. Keep your opponents away from the net by returning service low and cross-court to land at the feet of an incoming opponent.

101

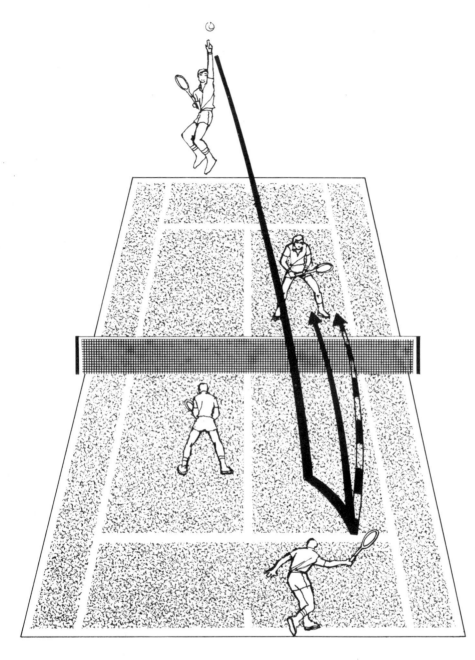

Figure 34 A useful alternative on service return is to attack the opposing net player by hitting the ball at them or low to the backhand.

As part of your communication plan, tell your partner whenever you intend to try something special or unusual on the serve, so that they will have a better idea of what to expect from the other side of the net.

Let me repeat this very important point about serve: be consistent. Aim to get your first serve into play almost every time by sacrificing power for accuracy. Once you have mastered the art of imparting spin or slice on your serve, use this, harnessed to good control, as your main weapon rather than brute force. An added advantage is that this type of serve clears the net — or should clear the net! — with feet to spare, thus giving you that desired high percentage of first serves.

By serving in this manner you should also be able to achieve the second requirement of doubles serving, getting the delivery in deep — within a yard of the service line and even closer if possible.

A deep serve will mean that the receiver's return has to travel farther, which gives you that extra fraction of time if you are moving in to volley, and it will also tend to force him to stay in a defensive position on or near the baseline. Consistent deep serving virtually ensures that the receiver's ambition is limited to little more than getting the ball back. If you are serving deep they are forced into a deep receiving position.

The direction of your serve is almost as important as the consistency. Aim at your opponent's weaker side, which almost invariably at club level means the backhand, varying the dose with the occasional wide serve to their strength or one hit straight at them. This variation will avoid any risk of helping an opponent to 'groove' his weaker side into a more effective weapon.

Now, what of your role when your partner is serving? There are a few

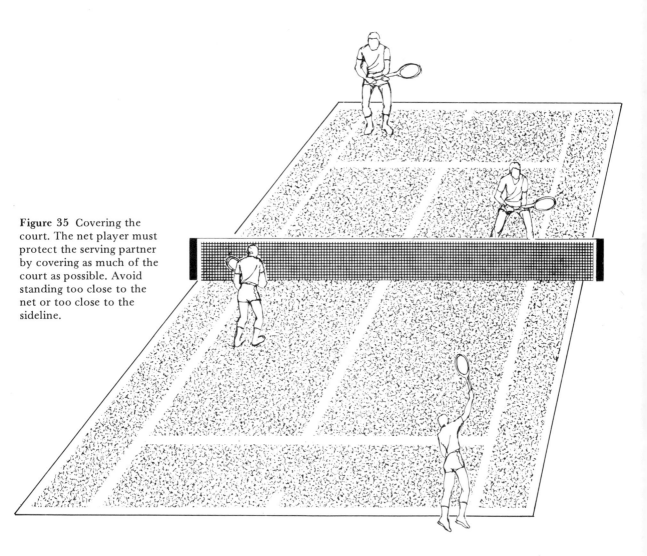

Figure 35 Covering the court. The net player must protect the serving partner by covering as much of the court as possible. Avoid standing too close to the net or too close to the sideline.

basic rules: first, be on your toes all the time because doubles is a quick-fire business. Never turn round to watch your partner preparing to serve. Not only is this off-putting to the server but it also deflects your own concentration from the job in hand, which is to keep your eyes fixed on the person receiving the serve. That is where the ball is supposed to go and, what's more important, that is where it will be coming back from, possibly in your direction and at a great rate of knots.

You should take up your stance roughly in the middle to fore-part of the service box, though you could stand closer if your partner is a good server, and perhaps a shade further back if you are facing an experienced returner of serve. It is perfectly legitimate to make the receiver well aware of the threat of your presence in that forward position. And there is nothing more calculated to worry him than the danger that you may be prepared to indulge in a spot of poaching.

Poaching is the name given to the act of crossing into your partner's side of the court in order to intercept your opponent's return at the net. Effective poaching can be valuable by keeping your opponents unbalanced and worried about the threat of your hurtling across the court to kill what would otherwise have been a perfectly good cross-court return to your partner.

You will find you can win quite a few easy points by pretending to poach, moving your upper torso as if preparing to move into your partner's side of the court. This can persuade the receiver to attempt an ambitious down-the-line shot, or dump the ball in the net in confusion and distraction, or end up by giving you a simple volley to the position he thought you were about to vacate.

To poach successfully, your timing must be precise. Don't make your move too early or you will leave your sideline exposed to the passing shot. Don't move too late, or your partner will still have to play the shot with the added distraction of finding that you have moved into his half of the court.

When you do manage to pull off a successful poach, the place to aim your volley is the vital area *between* your two opponents. Another good ploy is to aim at the opposing net man, who will generally be far too startled to do anything about it.

Whether you intend to poach or not, make sure that the opposition is always aware of the fact that you are standing up at the net. If they are thinking about you, they'll be worrying about you.

Next let's deal with the return of serve, which I consider possibly the most demanding stroke in doubles play. Here's why.

In receiving and returning the serve, you are actually playing on your own against two people. For that short space of time there's nothing at all your partner can do to assist you. Your skill and mental agility are being fully tested in conditions which favour your opponents.

If the opposing server is any good, he will be aiming for your weaker receiving side most of the time. And you will be returning the ball with the knowledge, not only that you have only half the court to return into but that any looseness of shot will be punished by the opposition net man.

So what do you do? You must rely heavily on accuracy in your stroke, otherwise the point is lost at once. You should also face up to the fact that if the serve was deep and well placed, the best shot you can play is unlikely to be anything more ambitious than a good, defensive return.

Your shot will be a crosscourt one, unless you catch the server's partner badly positioned or attempting to poach too early. Your crosscourt should be shallow, intended to bounce near the service line if the server is coming to the net and thus forcing him to volley up or even half-volley. If he stays back, you can then hit a full backhand crosscourt return deep to the baseline, just as you would in singles, but angled enough to pull your opponent wide and give your partner the chance of an easy volley from his stretched return.

Whatever you do, try not to play your partner into trouble. Don't send back an easy return because all they'll get out of it is a bruised leg!

If your opponent's serve is a real 'beaut' you will probably be able to do no more than stick your racket in its line of flight. This is known as blocking the ball, and is infinitely better than trying a violent swing in return. You will be feeding off the server's pace and could be pleasantly surprised by the outcome with a bit of luck.

Against a less ferocious serve the shot best guaranteed to skim the net and land near the service line is an abbreviated return, known as a 'chipped' shot. To play it, you employ a swing which is midway between a volley and a full ground stroke, hitting through and under the ball. You should also step forward into the ball more than you would normally, thus cutting out the risk of sending a high floater over the net by hitting up on the ball.

Against an impetuous poacher, you will be able to score a winner or two with returns down the line, or even the occasional lob. This can be devastating against a net-rushing pair.

Always be prepared to run around a second serve. You should generally have time to line up a forehand return to a second serve projected at your backhand in the deuce court, but it is much riskier to attempt this in the ad court, where the serve aimed at your backhand is pulling you out of court anyway. To run even further out of court in order to bring your forehand into play could be downright foolish.

Now the volley. As I mentioned at the start of this section on doubles technique, a good volley is essential in order to progress to your full potential. If you want your doubles to be enjoyable and diversified, you must develop the volley.

The distance from the baseline to the service line is 18 feet, but with reasonable reflexes and fitness you will find yourself able to traverse that distance as you go in behind a serve or a good, deep ground stroke. But beware of the phrase 'to rush the net'. Too many people interpret this literally and go charging right up to the net itself. In this exposed position, against opponents with time to make a choice, you could be picked off with a passing shot, a deep lob or a shot directed straight at you. The watchword with the volley is: keep your distance. Except, that is, when you go in for an easy kill.

Angles are important in doubles volleying. On the easier volleys you should always attempt to hit an angled shot in order to manoeuvre an

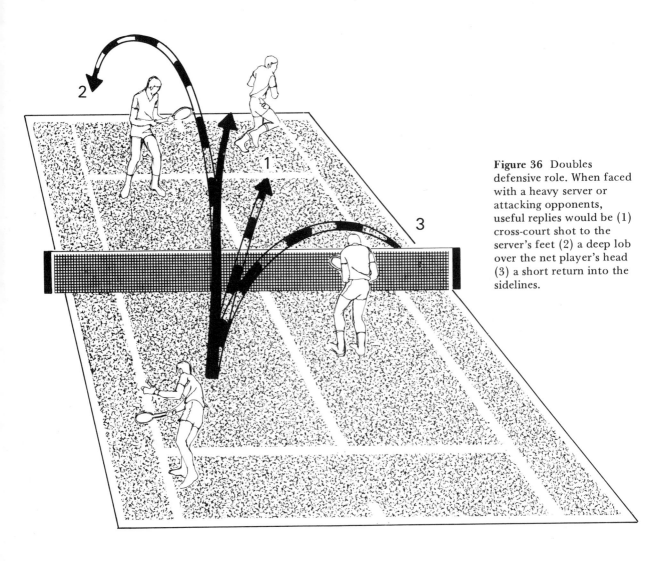

Figure 36 Doubles defensive role. When faced with a heavy server or attacking opponents, useful replies would be (1) cross-court shot to the server's feet (2) a deep lob over the net player's head (3) a short return into the sidelines.

opening, but if you notice that your opponents don't possess too much team work and understanding hit a few straight down the middle to confuse them about which one should be trying to return the ball.

For the rest, the volley is made in much the same way as in singles, with the exception that you are aiming into a better covered area so you must be accurate. Keep your eye firmly on the ball, keep the stroke short, simple but firm and resist the temptation to apply 'overkill' to what looks like a simple volley. Recognise the low volley for what it is at any level of tennis, a difficult shot that needs careful handling.

In doubles, the lob is used more frequently than in singles. Although the softest of shots, it can have the most devastating of effects as an attacking, defensive or simply change of pace stroke. I have already discussed how the lob can be utilised as a straightforward return of serve against opponents who favour the net. It can cause all sorts of confusion in the other camp. They have to cross over, the server has to chase it, and while they're doing this you and your partner can move in and take

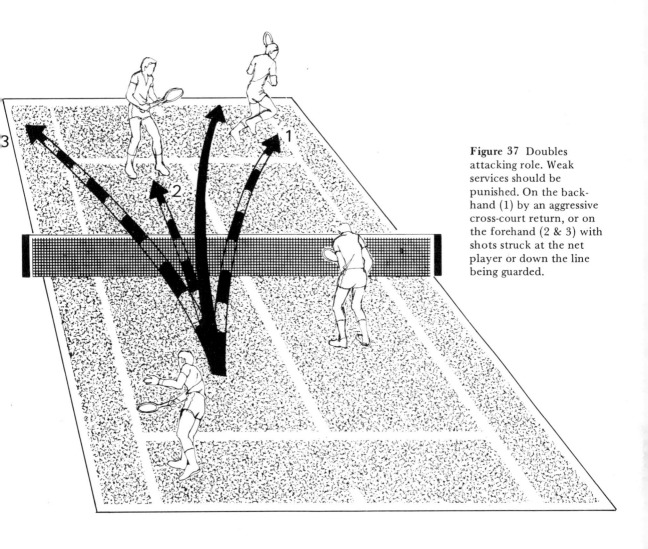

Figure 37 Doubles attacking role. Weak services should be punished. On the backhand (1) by an aggressive cross-court return, or on the forehand (2 & 3) with shots struck at the net player or down the line being guarded.

the net position, the most important thing in doubles. All this with only one shot!

Try to aim your lob over the opposing net man's backhand side. This will increase the difficulty in returning it positively. But don't forget to give the lob plenty of follow-through, otherwise you will lob short, and by now you should know what that means . . . .

Yes, the smash. This stroke, too, is used with much more frequency than in singles. I am sure you have at some time seen, in professional play, one pair putting up a succession of lobs while the opposing partnership replies with a stream of smashes until either one lobs short or the other smashes out or into the net.

To avoid losing the point on a smash — something you should hardly ever do — aim it either at the feet of the opposing net man if he hasn't had the sense to vacate his advanced position, or punch it straight down the middle of the court if both opponents have scuttled back to the baseline.

TACTICS

Be smart. That's the first piece of tactical advice, because doubles really *is* a battle of wits. It's you and your partner against another pair and the team best able to sort out quickly the opposition's strengths and weaknesses is going to come out on the right side of the match result. I know that I *really* have to think out the points more than most, because I rely on my return of serve and back court play rather than serve and volley.

The ability to analyse the opposition is part of that indefinable quality known as teamwork. You're a partnership and that's the way you should plan to move, side by side to the net whenever possible, or back together at the baseline if necessary. Try hard to preserve a balance between yourselves. Don't let gaps appear. This can be a danger when one player is temporarily reduced to the role of spectator and his sharpness is dulled. This is where the ability to 'lift' your partner's game is vital.

Because of the very fact that you are operating as a team, it can be a blow to the morale of one of its members if he considers that he has let down his partner with a weak volley, wild return or poor second serve on an important point. This is when you must be careful, no matter what your inner feelings, to encourage your partner for the next point, or the next game, with some cheerful comment or piece of advice which will help them forget the awfulness of their error.

Be brief, otherwise it might sound like a lecture or an impromptu lesson. Crack a joke if you think it will be appreciated. But be at pains to reassure your partner that you still have faith in his ability.

On no account should you ever criticise — after all, you may be the one to drop the next clanger. Avoid at all costs frowning, groaning, tut-tutting, shaking your head or any form of cutting comment. If you are tempted — and it's undeniable that the temptation is often there — just stop and think how *you* would feel if it was being done to you. And also think what a boost it is to the opposition to hear the pair of you grumbling at each other. A divided team is a beaten team.

You should also try to avoid apologising to each other too much if things do go wrong. If you know your partner, you will appreciate that he is aware how bad you feel after you have dragged a smash into the bottom of the net. It wasn't a deliberate mistake. There are more points scored on errors than on winners in tennis, so if you said 'sorry' every time you did something wrong he could soon be sorry you were operating as a team.

Beware of self-consciousness when playing with a more competent partner. There's nothing he can do to help you when you are playing your strokes, so make sure determination takes precedence over embarrassment. A good opposing team is bound to concentrate its attack on you in this case, so a few winners will be much more welcome than a steady chorus of 'sorrys'.

Having discussed how to eliminate divisiveness in your own camp, let's turn to the methods of exposing weaknesses across the net. Remember, there are two sets of weaknesses to work on and if player A looks a lot more vulnerable than player B, don't waste any time getting to work on proving it.

Never commit a double fault against the weaker opponent, and never let the weak one get away with a 'dolly' second serve. By punishing this sort of shot you can lay the groundwork for unhinging your opponent's co-ordination and, possibly co-operation.

Against a couple who haven't operated as a team before, try a few shots down the middle. This could quickly undermine their teamwork as they try to make up their minds whose responsibility it was for missing the ball. And if they start to bicker, all is lost!

Don't harbour any doubts about attacking the weaker opponent, by the way. It's not gamesmanship at all, merely a sensible method of winning the match. After all, *you* aren't responsible for that particular player being on court. So zero in on the weaker player, and just by way of underlining their deficiencies, and possibly exacerbating any ill-feeling, hammer your point-winning shot past the more accomplished opponent.

I have already mentioned the need to hold regular communication with your partner. There are so many things you can discuss to establish a better understanding. And these frequent little conversations can be another nail in the coffin of a divided opposition. They will be thinking to themselves 'what on earth are they discussing now?' as you pause for a brief chat before moving into position.

Your partnership will be strengthened by coming to an early agreement about who plays which side of the court. Whichever of you has the stronger forehand should normally play in the right hand, or deuce, court, while if you are lucky enough to have a partner with a good backhand the left side, or ad, court is without doubt the place for him. If your partner is a left-hander he, too, should take the left-hand court, which should make your team formidable on both wings.

There are some good examples in the pro ranks of excellent left-right combinations, such as John Newcombe and Tony Roche or, more recently, Peter Fleming and John McEnroe.

If you are both right-handers, however, the right court player has more opportunity to bring into play his strong forehand and therefore become the aggressive, or point-winning, partner, while the left court player needs to be consistent in returning the stuff that will be aimed at his backhand.

As the player at the net your duty is to cover your side of the court from net to baseline. You can best do this by positioning yourself roughly in the centre to fore-part of the service box which gives you the best chance of reacting well to most combinations of shot directed into your half.

Just as you should place the stronger forehand in the right hand court, so you should always get the better server to open for your team. And if you win the toss, choose to serve first. This is much more important in doubles than singles, because the advantage of serving is much greater.

Against opponents who are particularly strong at cross-court returns or rather deadly at lobbing, it is sometimes worth trying out what is known as the Australian (or tandem) serving formation. This involves the net man positioning himself in the same half of the court as the server, in other words directly in front of his partner.

For this formation the server should stand close to the centre point of the baseline in order to be able to move quickly into the empty half of the court and deal with the down-the-line return. In addition to these tactical advantages, the tandem formation can easily confuse opponents who are not accustomed to dealing with the unusual.

You can also adopt an unorthodox position to receive serve, in which both you and your partner are positioned on or near the baseline. This is a tactic worth trying if you are being overpowered by the serve and volley game or falling victim to an athletic poacher. By standing deep you force the opposition to alter the depth and angles of their volleys, with the chance of inducing a few errors from this change of pace and rhythm.

When your partner is receiving serve you should, in any case, stand further back from the net than the opposing net man. A couple of feet in front of the service line, I'd suggest. That will give you a split-second extra to react to a volley directed your way, and will also put you in a good position to call the serve, something which is needed in normal club play with its lack of officials.

Move a little nearer the net as your partner prepares to receive a second serve. You should always be aggressive when facing a second serve, but the receiver must not allow himself to become rooted to the spot against a slow serve. Move the feet, get into position and hammer it, not wildly but with calculated venom.

Finally, a tactical reminder about poaching. When your partner moves into your half of the court on a poaching mission, your job is immediately to get yourself to the untenanted side of the court into which your opponents will be returning the ball if the poach is not completely successful.

MIXED DOUBLES

If I was a club player mixed doubles is what I'd play most of the time. For a start it can only improve a woman's game, because you get the opportunity to return a man's serve. It's a bigger challenge. And if you succeed it makes your day!

I think the men enjoy it more too, because they can have a little bit of fun, and that's what people are playing the game for. I know that the aim is to improve your game, but you should have fun doing it.

The biggest talking point in mixed doubles, and the question I get asked most often about is, should men ease up when serving to or hitting at the woman on the other side of the net? Well, maybe in club tennis it might save arguments or ill-feeling to do so but if I was playing mixed doubles I would feel a little bit insulted if anyone did it against me.

If you are a true competitor you want to beat anyone when they are trying their hardest and playing their best. To hear it said that you only won because so-and-so was being kind is not pleasant.

I wouldn't want that, I would want them to try to knock me off the court. Then if you win the match you know you have won it because you are the better team.

There is no doubt that if you don't direct your attack at the weaker partner in a doubles (as I have already mentioned) you are wasting a legitimate opportunity to dominate and win the match. But having said that I should add that it does depend on the level of play. It would be bad form for an experienced male to bombard a woman beginner as she stands petrified at the net, especially if it's only a friendly club occasion.

Fear of being at the net is something that ought to be overcome if you want fully to enjoy your mixed doubles occasions. It is also important to overcome any inferior or defeatist attitude, the idea that the woman is only on court to make up the numbers. By all means discuss any weaknesses you feel you may have, so that your partner will be prepared to make adjustments to his own game if necessary, but don't for heaven's sake go out there with the idea that you ought to leave as much of the work as possible to the man.

This does not mean that a mixed doubles should not use the man's superior strength to the best advantage — of course you should. For instance, the man should serve first unless there is some particular weather factor, such as a strong following wind, which makes it preferable to let the woman open the serving.

Unlike men's or women's doubles, where the stronger hitter takes the right hand court, in mixed doubles the woman usually takes this position while the man moves into the left hand court, since close games are usually decided here.

Since men are generally better overhead, it is probably preferable that they deal with the lobs (which, incidentally, tend to proliferate in mixed doubles). But it's best to get the woman's agreement to this beforehand, so that there is no risk of her feeling miffed or out of it. Likewise if the male partner likes to hurl himself around at the net and do a lot of poaching.

In conclusion, girls, as you attempt to deal with the shots being fired at you by that big brute across the net just keep calm, get the ball back and remember that in doubles it is accuracy, and not power, that is more important.

15. Practice

Practice is an unavoidable part of learning the game of tennis. When you are starting out you simply have to go through all the exercises, no matter how boring they may seem. It's a bit like learning to play the piano and doing all the finger exercises.

Don't worry if you have no regular access to a court. Many of the leading players develop their skills in simple ways, such as hitting a ball against the nearest available wall. As a youngster I never had a proper practice wall in my area, so I used to hit up against the back of the garage at our home in Paignton. It had cracks in it so I used to get all sorts of weird bounces, which helps to sharpen your reflexes even more and there was also a pipe down the middle which made me hit from one side to the other. But it is better to hit against a wall with a plain surface whenever possible.

This sort of practice is particularly useful for volleying, because you get a low ball coming back at you very quickly, and it is not easy to find an opponent good enough to give you close volleys at the net on an actual court.

Always bear in mind that tennis is a game of movement and remember to keep hitting the ball at angles so that you will be forced to move for the return bounce. Hitting the ball straight at the wall time after time will, of course, help you to get the feel of the racket and to build confidence but moving your feet and body to reach a return from the wall is important, too. Also have a target to aim at on the wall. Chalk a couple of circles about four feet apart and aim at them alternately.

The practice wall is a valuable time to develop your rhythm, and that other key factor — watching the ball right onto the strings of the racket. One of the most common faults in tennis is lifting your head to see where the ball will be going before you have actually struck it. So remember, keep your head down and watch *every* ball right onto the strings. A serious and elementary mistake, such as lifting your head and taking your eye off the ball, will be doubly hard to eradicate later.

When you *do* get onto a court to practise, make sure that you make the maximum use of every minute. At every practice you should try to put yourself into the frame of mind of playing a match. It's your big chance to work on every shot you are going to try in the match. Hit a hundred forehands down the line, then a hundred backhands. Then hit a hundred forehands across court, and a hundred backhands across court, until you feel you could hit a hundred examples of *any* shot without missing one. Subsequently when you walk on court for the real thing you have no excuse for saying 'Oh, I haven't tried that shot yet'. Even if you are a baseliner, use the opportunity to get up to the net and sharpen your volleying.

Only when you have worked thoroughly on the basics can you become more adventurous in your practice drills. Once the basics have been sorted out, variety is essential. Some people go out and practise their drills faithfully but when they get into a match and are suddenly faced with one short ball, then a long one, they literally don't know whether they are coming or going.

The remedy for this is to play as many practice sets as time permits. After your drills, for instance, finish with a set of tennis, playing for points. That's the ultimate object, after all. You can drill as much as you like but you are only going to be a good tennis player if you can win matches.

Now for some useful practice exercises. One which I always like is to have the person playing against you to have the freedom to hit the ball anywhere on your side of the net while you are confined to a regular routine of returning two consecutive balls to their forehand, then two to their backhand. This means that, although you have no idea where the next shot is coming at *you*, you know exactly where you have to return the ball at *them*. This is an excellent discipline and makes you mentally alert. You go for your shot with an exact picture already in your mind about where you are going to hit it — which is what you have to do in a match.

For those whose practice time is limited, and that means the great majority unfortunately, concentrating on combining those vital drills with proper point-winning play, as I have already described, but with 'punishment points' designed to eliminate weaknesses.

For example, it you keep hitting the ball into the net force yourself to strike it higher by losing *two* points every time you commit this fault. And do the same thing if you keep lofting the ball beyond the baseline. If you are double faulting too often play a number of games in which you are allowed only one serve.

Concentration in tennis is really vital, and whenever you watch the top players, men or women, you will quickly be aware that they are totally absorbed in what they are doing.

One good drill designed to improve concentration is to aim your shot for a designated spot on the court. If you have problems with accuracy put a racket cover or tennis bag on the court and hit at it to help you gain accuracy. The chosen spot should always be a few feet inside the lines to allow for error. If you are thinking that every shot ought to hit that chosen object you will find that your concentration really improves. After a while you won't need the racket cover or bag, because you will already have a mental picture of where you want to hit the ball.

Always keep setting yourself different targets, always work hard to eliminate a certain error. You may never be able to play a perfect game but it should never be from lack of trying.

Practice must not only be something that you do a lot of, but it must be something you enjoy. When learning tennis you should aim to practise at least four times as much as you actually play. I compete in more tournaments than most other players and I *still* practise tons more than I play matches. But remember, it must be constructive practice.

It is said that a champion can adjust to any court, but for children or others learning the game a slower court is much easier. If you have a choice between clay and grass for instance, pick clay for your practice. The slower surface gives you more time to know what you are doing and to see the ball.

But don't forget that to practise your game you don't necessarily need a net or an opponent. I used to play in the road, but I know that is not advisable these days. Still you could always find a pathway or something which is traffic-free. I even used to play a form of volley tennis on the beach with my brother in summertime. It teaches you accuracy, because every time you miss you have to run a mile to retrieve the ball.

Tennis machines are popular in the United States for practising, but I am not in favour of them because once you have returned the initial delivery you don't get the ball back again. I have found that there is always someone who wants to play tennis with you.

And don't forget that important fitness rule: do about 20 minutes of stretches and exercises before playing, especially if it is cold weather, because you often get muscle pulls in those conditions. A few simple exercises before playing is good for you and your tennis.

16. The Mental Approach

If your body has to be fit to play tennis, so does your mind. You can't go out and perform at your best when you are tired, for instance, if you want to improve. A good match brain and a good temperament are vital.

Tennis *is* mental, it is what you *believe* you can do, it is having confidence in yourself. I firmly believe that tennis is more than 80 per cent mental. Technique is obviously very important, but there are no two top players in the world who hit their shots alike.

There are the basic shots of tennis, which is what we are discussing in this book, but everybody has his or her own way of hitting a shot. I can't stress too heavily that you should always play to what feels natural to you. Technique is important, of course, but the mental approach is much more important. Your own attitude is crucial.

Let's take the matter of temperament first. When I first started in tennis everything was obviously new to me, everything was a challenge. In the beginning you are always keen to go out there and play, no matter what the conditions of your own mind, or the weather, or anything else. That's a big problem with people when they are starting out. It's great to get out on the court and have a lot of fun. And why not? But it's a lot more fun winning. Nowadays when I play it's a matter of trying to do better every time, a conscious and totally different approach. Avoid mistakes. Improve. These should be your aims.

If you always seem to get beaten in close matches, for instance, stop and think about it. Analyse the strokes that are letting you down and work on them, but remember that your mind must *always* be active in a match, even if you are a set and 4-2 up. Every point should still be as vital as when you started the match. You must always be working for that victory.

Avoid being one of those people who feel that their game will work less efficiently in hot weather or a cold wind, or on a surface which is slow or fast, or against a certain type of player. Try to make it a basic attitude towards tennis that nothing like this can put you off your game.

There is much to be gained from studying your opponent before and during a match. It has been said that you should hate your opponent, but I don't agree with that. I could never actively hate someone on the other side of the net. I certainly wouldn't do them any favours, mind you, but that's different from hatred. Simply remember that most of the battle is against yourself.

Never be too conscious about playing someone special. For example, if I faced Billie Jean King and was conscious of the great things she has done in her career I probably wouldn't be able to hit a ball over the net for thinking about it all. You should always be playing the ball, playing the court, playing tennis to the best of your ability, no matter who your opponent is.

If you are facing your jinx opponent — and everybody has one — you *must* try to forget this and just get on with the match. Don't ever let the will to win slip away. Remember that victory probably looks just as far off to your opponent as it may do to you, and *concentrate*.

You need to concentrate for every second of the match, not only on every single point, but between rallies too. That's when distractions can intervene. Good concentration can bring you a first set score of 6-2, but a lapse that costs a service break hands them the second set 6-4. So you are back where you started.

If the opportunity arises, it is important to study your opponent before you play. But be careful to watch them *constructively*. Study how many forehands they hit before they miss one, which direction they hit the majority of forehands and backhands, what they do off a short ball, where they serve most of their deliveries and if there is ever a difference in their service throw-up. There are so many things to look for — how many drop shots they try, for instance, or whether they like to pass a net player down the line or across court.

Then, when you walk on court against that player, you will have a mental idea about how to play the match before the first ball is struck. You will know which way you will need to move, rather than just being surprised at losing the first six games. It's a little late to be learning after you have dropped the first set.

Another important thing to watch for in your opponent is their reaction to your own best shot. Watch where they return that shot, and be prepared for that reaction.

Obviously you should concentrate your attack on your opponent's weakness, but don't hit *every* shot to that weakness. If you keep on doing that they will get stronger. If you are 30-love up, for instance, don't hit to that weaker backhand side. Save it for when you are 30-40 down, when the point is really important.

My own game is a case in point. When my backhand was bad so many people hit so many balls to it that now it has become a very reliable shot. It got so much more practice than any other department of my game that it simply *had* to get better!

You can learn a lot, by the way, from watching people other than those you will probably be playing against. When I was younger I decided my game was a bit limited and I didn't have a lot of ideas about how to improve. So by watching different players hit their shots I decided 'I could try that'. Always remember that. You're never perfect, there's always something you can learn by watching the way others do it.

Nerves clearly play a big part in your mental approach to the game. But try to remember that it's usually a case of excitement rather than sheer nervousness. It's the challenge, the uncertainty of it all which is

A fine example of total concentration on the task in hand.

affecting you. As long as you realise that all should be well. Nervousness at the start of a match should disappear after two or three games. If you can't get rid of it after that sort of time spell, then you're in trouble.

For my own part, I know that if I *wasn't* nervous before a match I wouldn't play well. If I am not nervous that's it, I might as well forget it, because in my case the nervousness gets the adrenalin going. Playing in front of an audience for the first time may affect you, for example. Or your parents or friends may be watching. I know that the first time I played in front of a big crowd I was nervous all the way through the match. I never relaxed and I was terrible. You simply must overcome situations like that. OK, you hated it, but you must push yourself to go out and do it again.

Having been slaughtered that first time in front of a big crowd I dreaded the next occasion but I had to face up to it. Now it doesn't bother me to play in front of 10,000 people. My only nervousness is concerned with whether I am going to do well.

If it is important to control nervousness, it is absolutely vital to eradicate any signs of temper. Never, *never* lose your temper. It is the most heartening thing for your opponent to watch you throw away your racket or swear or something. If I was playing someone and they did that, I would

Don't be afraid to improvise if you don't have the time for the composed stroke.

know they were really worried and it would make me feel much more confident.

If your opponent loses his temper that's your cue to move in and finish him off while his mind is in a turmoil.

When I was learning the game I often used to get really angry with myself if things didn't go right and my coach Arthur Roberts was quick to point out to me what a potentially damaging thing this could be.

Although it is a reflex thing and you invariably regret it afterwards, you have to try really, really hard to avoid losing your temper. If you fail to keep your temper, punish yourself for it. If you have a coach, get him to administer some form of punishment. It really is important.

Mr. Roberts used to stop me playing and send me home. He used to make me feel really small and say 'You've let yourself down, you've let me down and you've let your family down. Do you really think your parents would want to see you behaving like this? Go home until you've learned more sense'.

I know very well that it's a difficult thing to stop yourself sometimes, particularly when you are mentally keyed up for a vital point, but just remember that as soon as you throw your racket to the floor you will regret it. And then you only have to pick it up again, anyway. You might as well save the energy.

Try to model your temperament on someone like Chris Evert or Bjorn Borg. They probably have the best mental attitude of any top players. They rarely show any sort of emotion, never let their opponents know what they are thinking. In Chris's case, she always looks so calm that you never feel as if you have begun to get on top of her.

Getting annoyed with officials is something else which has no future. It has happened to me quite a bit, but eventually you have to realise there is nothing you can do about it, and is only another signal to your opponent that you are worried. After all, it's only one point and it's not the end of the match — unless it is match point of course! — so try to accept that officials are doing the job to the best of their ability and usually they have a better view than you do. You are seeing a moving ball and your mind is concentrating on where you are hitting it. Their job is to watch where it bounces. It is wiser to accept their decision.

A final word of advice. Try to keep calm at all times. If you start getting ruffled, you start rushing your game. And you will lose.

17. Sportsmanship

I suppose a rough definition of sportsmanship is someone who abides by the rules, while gamesmanship is a 'soft' way of cheating. Once gamesmanship was rather a jolly thing. There was even a book on gamesmanship which was subtitled 'How to beat your friends without actually cheating' and attempted to pass the whole thing off as a laughing matter. It has long since become much more serious, and now everything designed to put your opponent off his game comes under the heading of gamesmanship. In other words, cheating.

The rules of tennis, indeed of any sport, were framed to help people enjoy the game, not to stop cheating, but these days, certainly in the professional game, they have to be applied constantly to bear down on bad behaviour. Television, which has done much to spread interest in the game in Britain, particularly during its annual coverage of Wimbledon, has also unfortunately helped to spread the 'cult' of gamesmanship by zeroing in on the antics of a few people whose names need no mentioning. These days the book shops, particularly those in the United States, are bulging with learned volumes on how to win at all costs at tennis, or how to develop the 'killer' instinct. And a lot of their advice amounts to little more than gamesmanship.

I was brought up, both at home and on the tennis court, in very disciplined fashion and was never allowed to indulge in anything vaguely approaching gamesmanship. I was also brought up with the idea of not getting ruffled on court — or trying not to! — which is the best antidote to those who try to put one over on you. But there is no denying that gamesmanship and the sort of behaviour associated with it has won a lot of people a lot of points. And I must confess that there have been times when people using it have bothered me, so there is sometimes an advantage to be gained from it, I'm sure.

Sportsmanship consists of quite small and simple things on and off court. Be friendly with your clubmates and opponents. Don't love them to the point of losing, but actually 'hating' an opponent is something I could never do. You should always be willing to play tennis with anybody who asks. Don't be too haughty around the clubhouse, and don't be intimidated either if you find yourself in a foursome which includes the club champion. Being prepared to concede a point, or a let, when there is doubt is another sign of sportsmanship, though you should beware of being over-generous if your opponent is a gamesman — or gameswoman!

The attitude of the great Fred Perry is that tennis matches are to be won. I agree totally, but there are limits beyond which you should not venture in order to achieve those wins.

If you are ever tempted to indulge in gamesmanship, remember this: you are out there to play tennis. Gamesmanship doesn't give you a very good name, it doesn't look good and it doesn't make you any friends. I don't think there is any advantage to it, unless you really *want* to be lonely. The use of that form of cheating belittles you and, no matter how good a player he is, someone who resorts to gamesmanship gets a reputation for that rather than acknowledgement of his ability.

As I have said, I simply don't agree with gamesmanship. To begin with, if I ever indulged in it I would find that it broke my own concentration. But there are those to whom it comes easy. And there is no denying that some players get away with a lot by resorting to it.

Let's have a look at the various, and more common, types of gamesmanship being practised these days.

First, arguing. Everybody gets a bad call now and then, and feels like arguing about it. At club level, where more often than not there is nobody to call the lines anyway, there is bound to be occasional disagreement about whether a ball bounced inside or outside the line. Don't get involved, but at the same time don't allow yourself to be browbeaten.

You may call a close ball 'out' and your opponent considers it was 'in'. If the disagreement looks like becoming protracted, settle for a 'let' rather than get involved in heated argument. But beware. If it happens again, be firm. And don't be intimidated into agreeing to replay a shot which you are certain was good. React to any histrionics, such as arm waving, with cool, polite firmness. You could perhaps suggest, if it is a competition match, that you ask if there is anyone available to act as an umpire. But at all costs don't get drawn into any exchange of banter or more serious words. If such an incident has happened more than once, it is quite obvious that your opponent's intention is to break your concentration, to upset you. That should be avoided *at all costs*. I can't stress that enough, really.

I have often been the victim of an argument designed to upset me. While the argument has gone on I have been left standing at the baseline waiting to serve the next point. You should never stand still while such a dispute is going on. Walk around, keep thinking of the next point, keep your mind occupied, never listen to what is being said (or shouted!). And *never* go up and join in the argument, unless requested to do so by an official, but it is almost certain that the umpire has made his decision and is not likely to change it, especially under pressure.

Take comfort from the fact that it is going to upset your opponent even more if you simply pay no attention. Their aim is to rile you. Ignore them, and your concentration is preserved.

Time wasting is another familiar ploy of the gamesman. The most popular ways of wasting time are slowness at change-overs and dawdling between points. Or perhaps if you have settled into a winning groove your opponent needs to go off court to wipe the handle of his racket or to adjust some item of clothing. Don't react in any observable way. Never say or do anything, simply pretend it doesn't bother you. If you can show that it's not having the slightest effect, they'll stop doing it because the interruptions are only damaging their own game.

The gamesman will sometimes indulge in quick serving, in other words pounding down a service when he notices that you aren't quite ready. If you are taken by surprise the first time and are too late to throw up a warning hand to indicate that you want the point started again, you must watch carefully for an attempted repetition.

When you see an opponent growling, cursing, complaining loudly, squabbling with anybody in sight, slamming balls into the backstop or out of court, or indulging in any similar form of stupidity, the advantage is yours. They will never win the match with that attitude of mind intruding on their concentration.

Though you must always be on the alert for gamesmanship, don't be *too* touchy about it. Otherwise you may find yourself labelling an opponent wrongly. For instance, I would classify bouncing the ball before serving as an irritating habit rather than gamesmanship. If you know the person, be mentally prepared for it. If you don't know them, well, there's no rule against it. If you are keeping active, up on your toes, always moving, it shouldn't bother you too much. If it does start getting to you, try doing it back to them.

Bear in mind, too, that it is also quite permissible to move around while your opponent is preparing to serve. Everybody indulges in this, and though it is designed to distract your opponent's eye and concentration, it can hardly be classed as gamesmanship. For one thing, it keeps you on your toes, nice and loose and ready to pounce on the serve.

If you think your opponent has a shaky second serve, move in about three strides in a noticeable fashion. That's OK, too. Look as if you are going to pounce on that second serve and you can hear their knees knocking.

As long as gamesmanship continues to win matches for some people there will be new ways invented of upsetting an opponent within the framework of the rules. But remember no incident can last long if you are determined to be no part of it. And that is the golden rule. Never get involved or upset.

18. Life as a Professional

Let me say at once that life as a tennis player is very exciting. If I went back ten years I would do exactly the same thing again. I have always really enjoyed my tennis career, even from the days of practising as a junior down in Torquay. Everything was always a challenge to me, and I used to set myself targets. I started off by aiming for junior titles and gradually built up until I was playing for my country or appearing at Wimbledon. There is always something to look forward to, always something you can improve, and when you achieve those targets you feel terrific.

The professional life presents people with a wonderful opportunity to travel and see the world, which is something I always wanted to do. Mind you, I should also add that if you want to live out of a suitcase and spend a lot of your time in launderettes, it is the *ideal* life!

You may gather from that comment that I don't consider the tennis professional's life as glamorous as a lot of people think. When I say that I have been to Australia seven times, round the world seven times, and that I'm travelling every week of the year it sounds super but it's really very lonely too.

I travel alone most of the time, and I really miss my family and my friends, because when you play at the top level in women's tennis the other girls are rivals rather than friends. Although you know them and you mix with them and eat with them the fact that they are competing against you for titles and prize money means that you just can't be close friends with the great majority. I have about three really close friends on the circuit and that's all, out of about 200 girls.

The most difficult years as a touring professional are the first two or three. It is then that most people find it tough.

Living in hotels all the time is very nice for the first year or so but after a while you get a bit sick of it, and you long to raid a refrigerator or just lounge in a chair in a comfortable living room. Most hotel rooms are pretty small and they are very lonely places. Many of them also look alike, and this is something which is also true of nearly every city in America. A couple of times on my travels, after a long and tiring journey, I have woken up in the morning and looked out of the window and haven't had a clue where I am. I have either had to get out my diary or ring down to reception and find out exactly what place I'm in. I know it's difficult to believe but it really does happen. All that travelling gets very monotonous.

Nowadays I only see my parents for about five or six weeks every year. That's not very much for me because I am a family girl and I miss them. But I have only felt *really* homesick about half a dozen times in the five years I have been touring on the women's circuit.

It is vital to acknowledge that you have to give up certain things. I had three years of making my official residence outside the United Kingdom, but I missed Britain so much that I just had to come back and settle here.

Although, as I have already said, the life is often a lonely one it is a simple matter to involve yourself so deeply in tennis that you don't notice it. This is how the pro's day goes, for instance.

After waking, you do your exercises for about an hour, then go and practise for an hour or two hours, depending on whether you have a match or not, then you have to fit in breakfast or lunch sometime, again depending on your match schedule. Then you may watch a friend, or a possible opponent, play, after which you have to prepare for your own match and get your equipment ready. Even though you are alone, there are plenty of things to occupy the mind if you are a dedicated professional.

And there are always the rewards, of course. In my case, satisfaction is the primary reward, but obviously there is so much more money in tennis now than there was ten years ago. When I first started travelling at the age of 15 I had to get financial support from my parents and Mr. Roberts. After a year or so I was able to support myself, which is a big achievement for someone who was still at school.

Then I opened a bank account and bought a car, I had this and I had that. As you make that sort of progress it is a wonderful feeling, to know that you didn't waste all those years of practice.

In my schoolgirl years I used to train in the morning before I went to school, then I used to practise during the lunch hour. After school it was straight over to the courts at the Palace Hotel for another couple of hours' practice. It used to take me about an hour to get home to Paignton, then I'd have a quick meal and start on my homework.

That was my normal weekday schedule. At weekends I used to pack a lunch — a pint of milk, a ham sandwich and a Mars bar — and spend the whole day at the Palace courts. After this sort of day I was so shattered that I never went out socially. I didn't go to a discotheque, for instance, until I was 21.

So there *are* sacrifices to be made, but your life isn't ruined because there are so many compensations. For instance, I feel as if I've done something with my life, something money can't buy.

You don't have to be a rich person, either to play tennis or be a winner at tennis. Success at high level in a sport is a feeling that's totally different from anything else — different from passing your exams, or getting your degree, or getting married. You have done something for yourself that no one else could do. People help you, of course, like Mr. Roberts helped me. I couldn't have been a successful player without him. But it all came from my body. It is something that you yourself have created, and that is a very nice feeling.

I don't think you'd find any player who would regret going through what they had to in order to get to the top, not one person. If you can put up with the first couple of years the rest is pretty easy. My life is much easier now than it was three or four years ago. Now I'm not learning the game any more, I'm established and I've earned quite a bit of money. In fact I've earned as much as some people would make by working throughout their lives.

That's the bonus. In that short time I've achieved all that. That's my reward, too.

I would always recommend people to take up the tennis life — as long as they have the ability and the desire. In my own case I had to take the decision whether to become a pro or go to college and have a safe career. I chose to go to Australia and play their circuit. If things didn't go well, I would go back to university in two years. But as it turned

Life as a professional has its champagne moments and occasionally provides a chance to relax.

out I never needed to do that.

Always remember, too, that desire plays the vital part. As Mr. Roberts has always said, 'The more ability you have the less chance you've got of being a great player'.

I know this sounds strange, but in the women's game, apart from Evonne Goolagong and Martina Navratilova, the rest are pretty well manufactured players. The game didn't come naturally or particularly easily to them. So the odds are much more in favour of someone who didn't have that much natural ability.

Bjorn Borg and Jimmy Connors have natural ability of course. I'm not saying they haven't, but they are not as talented as someone like Ilie Nastase. All I am saying is that you don't have to have terrific natural talent to become a top player. I didn't! When I started I couldn't hit a backhand. You get there by practice and determination to prove that it can be done.

Index

132

A0004800020051